INCL. TASTY LOW CARB RECIPES!

LOW CARB

Diet

HOW WE LOST OVER 70 POUNDS WITHOUT GIVING UP FOOD WE LOVE

Jule Eisendick

LOW CARB DIET
How we lost over 70 pounds, without giving up food we love

Food is for eating, and good food is to be enjoyed... I think food is, actually, very beautiful in itself.
– Delia Smith

Low Carb Diet
Published by Breakthrough Ventures OÜ

All the information in this book is independent and combined carefully of the author and compiled and reviewed by the editor.

Nevertheless, content or factual errors are not excluded, which is why the publisher has all the information in the sense of the product liability declared without warranty. Neither the publisher still the authors can take liability on any substantive or factual errors.

Information or designation of companies, products or services are not to be seen as an advertisement but as a 3rd purely subjective ingredients of the author's choice for each recipe.

DEDICATION

I dedicate this book to my boyfriend who's always supporting me and eating everything I cook - from vegan recipes to unsweetened porridge, with enjoyment :)

I also dedicate this book to my grandmother (RIP) who inspired me with home-cooking and baking since my early childhood. If cooking skills can get transmitted via DNA, I know where I got it from <3

TABLE OF CONTENTS

BONUSES FOR YOU

What this book is about (and what it's, not)

Hey, my name is Jule and before we get started with Low Carb I like to introduce myself a little and like to talk about what this book is about and maybe even more importantly what it's not about.

First of all, this book will not lose the weight for you. However, the tips and advice in the book, will show you how you can change your eating behavior, so you can lose weight more easily.

This book is not about how to lose weight fast and quick, just to bounce back like a Yo-yo.

This book will show you how to start a new chapter of your life. The starting point into a new lifestyle and a long-term change in nutrition, without giving up on all the food you love.

This book is also not about how to suddenly look like a supermodel. But this book will help you to change your mindset about nutrition and find your individual healthy weight goal.

So if you are currently struggling with your weight or maybe even with health problems caused by wrong nutrition or overweight, this book can help you to move towards a healthier and lighter future.

Yes, you will hear many different thoughts and ideas about how to lose weight when you ask different people. Your body will even react differently than mine to special nutrition changes, so it is important to find your own way.

I never thought a lower carb diet would work for me, but now look at me, I'm writing this book and promoting an individual lower carb lifestyle...

Why, you ask? Because I tried too many diets before, and only this one is the only one that worked long-term. It made me hold my weight effortlessly, since a couple of years now. And if I would have listened to others I wouldn't be here. So always try and make your own experience and decisions.

If this sounds good to you, then I believe you will enjoy this book. And if you do, I'd love to hear from you and see your positive review on Amazon.

If you have any questions along the way, feel free to write us.

And if you feel like you could need a bit help to get started we offer personal 1-on-1 low carb coaching too.

This coaching will help you:
- to stay motivated, even when it gets tough
- to help you when getting caught by sugar cravings
- to help you make the change you desire, by holding you accountable

Low carb: "Cook yourself slim"

Introduction

"There's only one pleasure greater than the joy of eating well: It's the pleasure to cook well. "

-   Günter Grass

You might have faced this problem: You suddenly can't button the favourite jeans anymore, or the shirt that sat perfectly last month, no longer fit at all.

You tried countless diets in your life, but none has actually changed anything in the long run.

The motivation is gone and you just want to get back to bed to hide under the blanket?

No, please don't! Because there is a way to lose weight and stay healthy at the same time! The magic word is "Low carb"! It combines a low-carbohydrate-diet with a healthy lifestyle.
This way you will stay fit, lean and ahead of all: healthier!

Healthy eating doesn't mean you can only eat fruit, vegetables and whole grains.

While these should have a steady place in the meal plan, they are not the only main components. Meat (grass-fed, organic), fish and healthy fats play a big factor in a low carb diet too!

It is worth keeping an eye on the carbohydrates in your diet because this helps you to lose weight quick and healthy.

In the low-carb diet, the intake of carbohydrates is greatly reduced and protein and high-fat foods are increasingly permitted.

This is to ensure that the body gains its energy predominantly from fats and protein, instead of carbohydrates.

In this book, I would like to share with you how you can manage to change your life and, above all, your health with Low Carb.

On the next pages, you will learn interesting things about Low Carb and quickly realize how easy it is to enjoy healthy eating with joy and a new attitude to life.
You will learn what belongs in the shopping cart and what should stay in the supermarket

and also what kind of benefits the low carb diet can bring.

Healthy eating is easy when you know how to do it. And this is exactly what I want to show you in this guide!

Join me on a journey, to the pinnacle of enjoyment and learn to awaken a new refreshing way of life through Low Carb!

You will see, it will be worth it!

Our Low Carb Story

The couple in the picture shows my boyfriend and me. In the last few years, we gained a lot of weight.

And with a stunningly simple strategy, we managed to lose a little more than 70 pounds together in a very short time.

How we managed to do that, I'll tell you now ...

I (Jule) has always had this one dream: My own cafe. And in 2012, my long-awaited dream came true and I opened a cafe in Berlin. And from then on we practically sat at a "so-called cake source ." I baked everything myself (Jonathan: She bakes incredibly delicious cakes and perhaps the best cheesecake in town! So at least the best cheesecake I've ever eaten;)

And what happens to you when you sit at such a cake source?

Well, if you sit at such a delicious food source, then you use it too. And then you eat a little bit of cake here and there every day, sometimes a delicious muffin, or just a biscuit for coffee. If something was left over in the evening, we did not cook a salad or a vegetable stir fry at home but ate the homemade bagel sandwiches.

Throwing food away would also be totally against my mindset... Running a business all by myself didn't even allow me to do sports after work. A 7-day working week got me too exhausted and tired.

So over time, with too much wrong food and no exercise, we gained around 26-33 pounds. Each of us. The bad thing was: We barely noticed ... After all, you don't exactly increase 33 pounds overnight. Rather, it's a very slow process.

Time passed and everything was fine. But then one day something rather unusual happened ...

A Cafe guest and friend introduced my boyfriend to his buddy with something like this:

> *"May I introduce you? This is Jonathan.*
> *The café owner's chubby boyfriend ... "*

I was completely flabbergasted... And my boyfriend speechless and somewhat shocked. Had he just really said that?

Everyone probably had such moments in life when one suddenly realizes that something is wrong. These moments don't happen often, but when they come, then with a BIG BANG...

And for my boyfriend at that moment, that was his! In this case, he probably stood with his mouth open in front of the two of them for a long time.

Jonathan: "I wasn't really sure: Was this just a stupid saying? Or was there anything about it? After all, my mother had already said to me that I got a "belly". I hadn't found myself chubby, though."

So were they right then?

Either way, I found that remark quite cheeky. But the first stone started rolling ...

A few days later I had someone from the local newspaper with me who wanted to write about a social project I participated with called "Suspended Coffee " and of course he took a picture of me. When I saw this photo in the newspaper, I was caught by the realization: OMG, did I really gained so much weight?

On this day after work, I stepped on the dusty body weight scale for the first time in ages, and was shocked: 152 pounds. I had never weighed that much in my entire life. Now this may not sound much, but I'm not tall either...These two brief moments have brought us to immediate action.

I ruminated for a while, researched the internet and looked for really effective ways to lose weight on a healthy way without sacrifice... This is not a very easy task, because there are too many different understandings and believings when it comes to nutrition.

Some people say you need to eat nothing but apples. Or skip dinner. Or skip breakfast. Or eat more carbs and less fat. Others say eat as they did in the stone-age, heaps of meat in first place. Since I am vegetarian this was not the right nutrition for me.

To understand, you should know that I'm absolutely not a diet fan. Things like counting points or constantly juggling calories aren't mine. Or going to the gym excessively, I didn't feel like that either. And with my own store, I certainly had not enough time to spend a lot of time in the gym...

But quite frankly...

When I saw what some people had to restrict, I thought "Ok that's it. I am not going to do that..." Diets like where you can only eat "cabbage soups" or "apples" ...

I already had a phase in my mid-twenties where all these restriction diets led me into an eating disorder where I did not eat much, either healthy or enough, checking the body weight scale twice a day, and I definitely didn't want to go back.

There had to be something simpler and better and, above all, healthier ...

At some point, of course, I came across the low-carbohydrate-diet, or simply low carb. Somehow, that sounded exactly like what I was looking for. No excessive exercise, no hunger. Easy to integrate into my everyday life ... Only one thing: To give up fruit, to give up certain vegetables made me very sceptical at the beginning, but we just tried it anyway but somewhat with our own rules...

I created a low carb diet plan and after only 1.5 weeks the belly became much flatter (no more bloating), which of course was super pleasant, especially for my boyfriend.

And after only 4-5 weeks of low carb, the result was just WOW!

I had already lost about 11 pounds and my boyfriend 16.5 pounds. I suddenly needed a belt again so my favourite jeans didn't slip.

His blue favourite shirt, which he couldn't button before, fit perfectly again...

That was just amazing!

Meanwhile, we started to implement some running exercises, and I lost the gained 33 pounds (plus even an extra 4.5 pounds:) (my boyfriend also lost 33 pounds in total), and the best thing is that we had to restrict virtually nothing.

We always enjoyed oatmeal with fruit for breakfast, and also had pizza & Co.

You can find super good low carb version recipes for those.

My weight has now kept stable for 3 years straight, and I am not eating strictly low carb anymore. I treat myself to normal pizza or cakes in between. But I still don't eat much bread, pasta and rice on a regular basis. So there are actually no more excuses;-)

As a "reward " we treated ourselves to an overnight stay at the luxurious 5-star Hotel Ritz in Berlin because we had lost weight so quickly with low carb. Of course, with the finest restaurant visit! Here's the happy picture - 70 Pounds Less!

Low Carb Diet changed my life

I find it difficult to put into words what a grand feeling it was to be there and reward myself. 37.5 pounds lighter and twice as happy.

I'm noticeably more vital, my skin looks much better, I am more active and also more relaxed. And I never thought a lower-carbohydrate diet could have such an effect.

So you can say that I have had a great experience with low carb. Since that time, I am 100% sure that really anyone can lose weight with low carb too if he or she does it the right way.

By the way, it is known that with the time/age the metabolism is getting slower and slower, but I'm now in my late 30s and my metabolism has never been better.

I'm fitter and just as slim as I was in my mid-20s. And I'm actually eating healthier and more than ever. And even though I'm vegetarian, mostly plant-based and almost dairy free. I actually don't restrict myself from any favourite food anymore.

And the more we talked about our low carb journey with friends and relatives, the more often we were asked if we couldn't recommend good recipes or create nutrition plans so they could imitate it.

At first, we just did this for friends. But now would like to share our knowledge and "recipes for success" with you. So that you too can achieve your desired weight faster and easier than you thought.

We've packed all our knowledge, numerous tried and tested recipes, nutrition plans, shopping lists and more into this low carb diet book. This gives you a practical "guide " with which you will lose weight quickly "and tasty".

As you can see, I can say from my own experience: The Low carb diet can work. I tried it myself and quickly lost 37.5 pounds. If you follow the program, you can do it too.

In the meantime, more than 3,500 men and women have already followed our Low Carb diet and are now "cooking their belly fat" away. And it's great to see you taken on the journey for yourself!

3 Game-Changing Beliefs

Let them go & set yourself up for success...

Since the beginning of our lives, we've been adopting certain beliefs from our peers that helped us to navigate through life. A lot of those beliefs and behaviors have proven to be useful, like watching if a car comes, before crossing a street. Or to being nice to each other.

The belief we're talking about are rather limiting ones, especially the ones we tell ourselves. Here are some:

- I failed at a diet before, and I'll fail again
- I can't do that, because I'm too old
- It's easier for other people to lose weight
- I can't live without bread

In the self-help world we call these self-limiting beliefs also the self-fulfilling prophecies. Because the things you believe will determine your actions. And if your actions are focused on the things you can't or don't want, well, your subconscious mind will try it's best to prove you right.

Famous mathematician and physicist Albert Einstein once said, that the same thinking that brought us into this situation, won't help us getting out. So we need to change the thinking in order to change the results.

So if you want to change your results, it's time to let go of such limiting beliefs. It's time to set new positive ones.

Here are two more limiting beliefs, and hopefully an argument you can adapt.

"I can't do low carb, because this would mean I can't eat any carbs anymore in my life"

If you think like this, you'll certainly be intimidated, and you probably won't even get started with changing your nutrition for obvious reasons.

Nobody wants to miss his favourite bread or meal for the rest of his life.

But let me tell you this:

You don't need to let go of your favourite foods.

BUT consider eating them in moderation.

Low carb doesn't mean *NO carbs* for the rest of your life. It means, eat strict low carb in the beginning, but then eat *the right carbs* for the rest of your life. And everything else on special occasions and in moderation.

Birthday party?
Yes sure, enjoy a piece of cake! But not 3 ;)

Planned a hiking trip?
Yes, sure, pack some pasta salad or a sandwich.

Fancying a piece of chocolate?
Eat it and enjoy.

But do this maybe once a week, or every two weeks, and don't eat a entire bar of chocolate. Every. Day.

I guess you get where I'm going.

Here's also one for men...

"Low Carb is not the right diet for "real" men!"

This is similar to the vegetarian or vegan diet, were men often think: "It's not a men's diet", because they grew up with this thinking... and then they won't even try it, or join or support their women.

That's kinda sad, because the low carb diet (or even vegetarian, vegan diet) is a great diet for men, too. It will allow you eating more and combined with the right exercise help get rid of that "couch-potato-belly".

How you too can motivate or inspire your husband, boyfriend, or partner:

Sometimes it's hard to change habits on your own. It definitely helps to have help or support from family, partner, friends... If you have a resistant partner or family or friends, don't surrender. Here are a few ideas to get help from other people:

Groups: Join Low Carb groups or fitness meetups in your city. Search the internet and social media. If you can't find any, maybe try and start a group yourself.

Coaching: Another idea could be to get a coach who helps you to get started with that new lifestyle and will help you to stick to your plan and gives tips on how to stay on track over the first few weeks.

Whether that is a coach or friend you can meet in person, or a coach that supports you online through Emails, video chat, etc.

Chapter 1: What is Low Carb?

The Low Carb diet is a description for a long-term nutrition change that happens on a low carbohydrate diet.

Carbs, from pasta, bread, or rice, will be exchanged by various plants, proteins and fats. If you don't eat enough carbohydrates through food, the body changes its metabolism. Once the changeover has taken place, the energy is derived from fat reserves instead of carbohydrates. This changeover is called ketosis. Ketones are energy carriers that serve as alternative energy suppliers and force the body, so to speak, to use its own fat reserves as energy. This leads to weight loss.

If you eat foods with fewer carbs, the annoying carbohydrates cannot be converted directly into glucose and the body takes longer for processing carbs, which causes the feeling of satiety to last longer and you are less hungry.

Nutrition experts agree that low-carbohydrate eating successfully causes you to lose excess weight.
The food industry seduces us with cheap and convenient food, which is mostly calorie and carb loaded and drives thousands of people into excess weight. As a result, we are missing more and more high-quality carbohydrates, their vitamins, fibres and minerals that are particularly important for human health.

Low carb protects the pancreas, which is responsible for producing insulin. Carbohydrates that we know in "fast" foods lead to an ongoing level of insulin levels in the blood. As a result, our cells can only work with a high insulin dose and only slightly open up. Nutrients, therefore, have a very difficult time getting into the cells.

Important energies from the right food can no longer penetrate the working cells and the body runs on the minimal program. The nutrients are deposited in the fatty tissue and this will become bigger and bigger.

But how can this be prevented? Easy. With less and especially *the right* carbohydrates!

A low-carbohydrate diet is varied and provides you with all the necessary nutrients, in sufficient amounts. Low carb is becoming more and more popular and resonates with people all over the world.
The good thing is that low carb can be designed individually and therefore there is no "miracle recipe." There are various nutritional theories and diets on how to design a low-carbohydrate diet, making it easier to get rid of those extra pounds with enjoyment and delicious food.

I am gonna introduce you to four of the most well-known low carb nutritional theories in Chapter 2.

The difference between crash diets and a long term change in lifestyle

Just a few years ago it was clear if somebody is overweight the person needs to go on a diet. Today, however, there are other possibilities, namely the change in nutrition. But what exactly is the difference?

When dieting, you limit yourself temporarily in your food intake in order to quickly lose the excess kilos. Once you've reached your desired weight, it's just about keeping it. And that is precisely the well-known problem. Everyone knows the yo-yo effect and knows that it is almost impossible to maintain the desired weight when you finish the diet and start eating again as usual.

Changing your diet long term doesn't concentrate on a rapid weight reduction but in a long term change to a healthy diet. This will help to avoid the yo-yo effect. Unhealthy habits and behaviours will get detected and changed in such a way that you will find a more and more healthier and well-filling diet.

The advantage of a dietary change is that in the longer term, you can maintain your desired weight and it is healthier.

Losing weight quickly and effectively within 1 week is quite possible, but only really makes sense if the weight loss lasts sustainably. You don't want to have the pounds back on again quickly, do you?
Properly implemented, a permanent nutritional change keeps fit, lean and, above all, healthy.

It is important to learn a healthy diet that is satisfying, provides your body with necessary nutrients and that puts enjoyment back into the first row when it comes to eating. A change of diet means eating something else, or also, eating differently and not necessarily eating less.

If you manage to shed unhealthy eating habits and replace them with healthy meals, the energy intake will go down to a healthy level on its own. And all this without renunciation, but only through change.

A change in diet may take a little longer, but there is a marked improvement in well-being after just a few days.

If you want to achieve a permanent change in diet, the first priority is patience and discipline. You may not succeed if you force yourself to eat foods that you don't like just because you think it would be healthier. The change must take place in your mind first and then the body.

Only if you make small steps and find healthy foods that you really like, you can manage to change your diet in the long run in such a way that you also like it! Small goals will help you to notice the success quickly and build new motivation for the next step.
A slow change will eventually lead you to a diet that is both healthy and delicious!

Just stay tuned, focus and practice your patience. In the end, you'll realise the wait was worth it and you'll feel permanently more comfortable in your body.

What are carbohydrates?

Carbohydrates are important components in our diet and provide energy to the body. They are made up of sugar molecules and drive our muscles and brains. So you should never eat a very strict low carb diet in the long term. Yes, you should eat strictly low carb in the beginning, but when you reached your goal weight, start to include some healthy, natural carbs into your diet (like potatoes, pumpkin, buckwheat, lentils, beans, etc.). Because they are very important for your body functions.

Sugar molecule sounds very sweet but they're not always. There are also carbohydrates in foods that have no sweet taste. These include potatoes, rice, pasta, bread or cereals. However, we also find plenty of carbohydrates in fruit, due to the sugar contained.

In addition to fat, carbohydrates play an important role in meeting the energy requirements in the body. They are fuel for the brain and muscles and get directly through the blood into important cells of the body.

Carbohydrates are divided into three different groups based on their sugar building blocks.

Simple sugar: These include glucose and fructose

Double sugar: This includes household sugar, malt and milk sugar.

The first two sugar building blocks are mainly found in sweets. They do provide quick energy but no vitamins or minerals and therefore quickly shoot up the blood sugar level.

Complex sugar: Complex sugars are mainly found in whole grains, cereals, potatoes and legumes. The blood sugar level is only slowly rising due to these products, as the sugar chain structures have to be broken down before they are absorbed into the blood.

Carbohydrates must first be broken down into simple sugars, i.e. glucose, in the digestive tract before they enter the bloodstream. In order to split the double or complex sugars consumed with food into the simple sugar (glucose), the body uses various enzymes. Depending on how many molecules a carbohydrate is composed of, it takes longer or even shorter for the energy to be available to the body.

The brain, in particular, needs glucose to meet its energy needs. In addition, carbohydrates, for example, play a leading role in blood types as signalling and detective substances.

Carbohydrates:
The dangerous seducer

Carbohydrates are important for the human body, but only to a certain extent.

Most types of carbohydrates are rather useless and also can't wait to finally get into the body. These include sweets, sugar and sugary drinks, but also rice, white floured pasta, bread, cakes and pancakes. All these carbohydrate-rich foods force their way into the digestive tract, passing it quicker than the healthy foods, forcing the body to shoot out a good portion of insulin. This opens the cells and lets the nutrients into it. There is no room left for healthy nutrients and it is necessary to wait until the blood sugar level drops again.

What is not used by our body ends up in the fat tissue, which allows it to grow further and further. The insulin transports the sugar out of the blood so quickly that the blood sugar levels drop again quickly. Your body will get into hypoglycemia (low blood sugar).

And then the vicious cycle begins: In your brain, the alarm bells will ring, as the body cannot work without blood sugar. In order to balance the blood sugar level, the body really demands replenishment. As a result, adrenaline is getting released and this creates stress. This stress in most cases leads to a quick munchie. Most likely you will grab snacks that are full of sugar, such as muffins, a chocolate bar, lemonade or chips.

These dangerous seducers cause people to become more overweight and dissatisfied as the circulation with insulin and the cells will start all over again. The end of the story could be life-threatening obesity.

It is important to avoid products that only supply simple carbohydrates if you like to have a healthy weight for the long term.

The so-called "bad carbs" include:
- Pure sugar
- Honey
- Cakes
- Chocolate bars
- sweets

- Lemonade
- Undiluted fruit juices
- White flour (white bread, pizza dough, etc.)
- White rice
- etc.

Even milk has natural sugar too. (Cow milk: 8 oz milk=13,45g carbs)

The consumption of these foods should be restricted or avoided altogether.

In addition, large amounts of sweet fruits are also unhelpful in your dietary change. Sweet fruits should only be consumed in small bites. In small quantities and in moderation! Some would say: We should eat fruits as our ancestors did when they still lived in caves, they only had sugary fruits when they were in season...

Carbohydrates are only good if they are in their natural form. That means not the sugar in a processed juice but preferably a small amount of fresh sweet fruit.

The small portion of carbohydrates also provides you with the necessary vitamins and vital substances. These are all substances that keep our bodies going. They are needed by the metabolism to efficiently implement energy or are also useful for excreting undesirable substances. Fibre, for example, is very important for healthy digestion. And many people nowadays actually have a lack of fibres in their nutrition!!

The following foods can supply us with healthy carbohydrates on a regular basis:

Potatoes (combined with lots of vegetables)
Fresh legumes (peas, beans, lentils, sugar peas)
Wholemeal cereals (wholemeal bread, wholemeal rice, wholemeal flour, buckwheat flour)
Fruits (sour fruits are best, berries, apples, etc)

A low-carbohydrate diet is simple and does not involve any renunciation.
If you have these foods on your daily meal plan, you can eat a varied and yet healthy diet.

Even though it will be difficult at first, don't be seduced by the dangerous carbohydrates. They lead you into a vicious circle from which it is very hard to get back out.

The right fat doesn't make you fat

Low carb does not mean eating fat-free. Healthy fats are vital for our survival and shouldn't get restricted! When it started some years ago that some humans started to say: "Fat is unhealthy and makes you fat" people actually started to eat more carbs and more and more people started to suffer from overweight and obesity. Companies started to sell "low-fat" foods that are actually filled with sugar or sugar substitute to make sure there is no lack of taste. Yes, you should avoid unhealthy trans fats, but not every kind of fat is bad for you.

The right fat is not only supporting the taste of food but many components from which fats and oils are built have very important tasks in our bodies.

They serve to allow us to absorb vital fat-soluble vitamins from our foods into the body in the first place and build up the body cell walls. They also help the body transport cholesterol so that blood cholesterol levels can remain normal-value.

Many people believe fat is the actual "fat-maker." Studies, however, prove exactly the opposite. A low-fat diet that includes lots of carbohydrates makes people become overweight even faster.

You can only lose weight properly with a low carb diet if you eat proper low carb foods and pay attention to the right fat when it comes to fat.

These include:
- Nuts
- Seeds
- Rapeseed oil
- Olive oil
- Coconut
- Walnut or linseed oil
- Fish instead of meat
- Avocado and avocado oil

With the oils, please try and make sure that they are cold-pressed because then they have the most nutrients. Otherwise, these will be destroyed by the heat when it gets refined.

Fat should only ever be combined in conjunction with low-carbohydrate foods, such as tofu, low-fat fish or meat or protein-rich products such as eggs.

If you consume too many useless carbohydrates, the vicious circle begins, which makes you overweight. Combining carbohydrates with fat is even more unhealthy. When eating carbohydrates, the body sets free a large amount of insulin. The insulin is said to quickly destroy the incoming sugar component in the blood. The insulin thus sends the blood sugar into different body cells, which are then filled.

But not only the sugar will get into the cells, but also other energy components that are in the blood. This also includes fat components. The cells are "fed" and will grow quickly, end result: We are getting fatter and fatter.

However, if you take these fats with low-carbohydrate foods, they cannot be misdirected by insulin. They would set out to build up important cell walls in your brain and can also serve as a component of hormones.

Hormones are formed by special hormone-producing cells: These are found in glands in the pituitary gland, thyroid gland, adrenal gland and pancreatic islets.

Some hormones are formed by nerve cells, which are called neurohormones, or neuropeptides.

Essential fatty acids are needed for the structure of cells or cell membranes and for various metabolic processes. They control the absorption of fat from the gut, regulate fat metabolism and help lower elevated cholesterol levels.

Prepare your low carb meals with a consciously measured amount of oils, because this guarantees a good taste.

Fats serve as flavourers and brings out the various flavour of foods. The most important point, however, is that fat is vital for us to survive and should not be dispensed with at all!

Some components of the fat cannot be built up independently by the body, which is why it is essential to supply them to the body.

Forget the mistaken belief that fat makes you fat. Use the right fats in your dishes and you will realize how easy it is to lose pounds!

Types of fat

Fats are distinguished by their origin in animal and vegetable fats. Important components of fats are fatty acids. The number, as well as the type of fatty acids, determine the property of the fat and its meaning for the human body.

Regardless of the type of fat, each gram yields 9 calories of energy. As a result, fats are the most important energy suppliers. Because carbohydrates and protein provide only 4 calories of energy per gram.

Saturated and unsaturated fatty acids are also distinguished. The saturated fats, mostly hardened so-called trans fats, in meat and sausages, fries, biscuits and cookies, but also palm fats are generally described as unfavourable. Their main task is to provide energy. If you eat mainly these and in excess, they can affect the blood flow and thus the Vascular, cardiac and brain function negatively.

The unsaturated fatty acids from the diet are vital for the body because it cannot make them itself. They have health-promoting properties. For example, they have anti-inflammatory effects and reduce the risk of cardiovascular diseases.

Monounsaturated fatty acids such as the oleic acid in olive oil help maintain normal blood cholesterol levels. Other great products include avocados. Calorie-rich fatty fish such as salmon, herring, mackerel and tuna provide vital polyunsaturated fatty acids that the body itself cannot produce. Valuable herbal alternatives include soy, nuts, seeds and vegetable oils such as linseed, rapeseed, soy or walnut oil.

Unsaturated fatty acids are easier to digest because they are easier to get broken down by digestive enzymes than saturated fat. We distinguish between omega-3 fatty acids, which have a positive effect on the heart and vessels, and the omega-6 fatty acids, which help to unlock vitamins from fruits and vegetables for the body.

Omega 3 fatty acids are found in rapeseed oil, nuts, flaxseed, soy oil, salmon, mackerel or even tuna. These are very important and anti-inflammatory.

Omega 6 fatty acids are present in sunflower oil, margarine and also mayonnaise. Too much of those can have a inflammatory effect. Be careful though, because Omega 6 is in so many convenience products, so we mostly get too much of it. This can block the anti-inflammatory effect of Omega 3. So concentrate on getting more of the Omega 3. Swap sunflower oil with rapeseed or avocado oil, etc.

In order for the dietary fats to be utilized, they undergo a certain metabolism. This starts with fat digestion. The fats are broken down in the digestive tract to generate energy from it. Digestion begins in the stomach. The movements of the stomachs wall lead to a slimy consistency of the fats from the food. At the same time, they get dismantled. On the way to the small intestine, the fats ensure a release of the tissue hormone, which stimulates the pancreas to use digestive enzymes and stimulates the gallbladder to release bile acid.

Now the dietary fats will be divided into their individual constituents, releasing fatty acids that can get captured by the intestinal walls. In the intestinal wall, the fatty acids are packed into a shell and can only continue on their journey and enter the blood via the lymphatic vessels. The blood then transports the fatty acids to their targeted location in the body, from which cell energy is getting obtained.

Chapter 2: Why Low Carb?

Sick from the wrong diet

In 2016 almost 2 billion adults worldwide were overweight. And 340 million children aged 5-19 were overweight or obese, while from children under the age of 5 already 41 million were overweight or obese.

Altogether a third of the world population is overweight or obese (2016).... (Source: who.int)

It ranges from a slight harmless overweight to life-threatening, severe obesity. More people are actually dying from obesity than from underweight these days.

Worst of all, being overweight affects all ages from children to adults and keeps rising. It has nearly tripled since 1975.

Fast food, soft drinks, sweets and all the delicious ready meals are stuffed into us and no one thinks about exercise. The world is becoming more and more modern and our food development is getting worse. A natural and balanced diet counts less and less these days and sadly unhealthy food is almost always more expensive than healthy food.

Nowadays, people are blinded by a variety of offers in supermarkets. Durable canned food and a colourful amount of industrially packaged food try to catch people with colourful stickers and inscriptions such as "50% fruit content" or "healthy and delicious" and low-fat to sell something as healthy, but it's often anything but this.

The chemical additives that contain these foods may make you feel full quickly, but this is usually paid for with digestive problems or only a short saturating period.

A healthy diet includes sufficient vital substances consisting of various vitamins and enzymes. Without enzymes, no metabolism can take place and thus the "machine human-body" cannot function and breaks down. Vital substances in our nutrition are very important for our health. However, these can only be found in fresh and unprocessed foods.

The industry earns a lot of money from people who trust that they buy "healthy and delicious" when it's written on the front packaging.

Nutrition-related diseases in the world population are rising and being overweight or obese is seen at every corner.

The supposedly slimming "light" products we find in the supermarket contain less fat but are full of sugar or sugar substitutes to maintain the flavour and often have more calories as a result. If manufacturers don't use sugar, they often use salt or synthetic sweeteners. At the end of the story, you will find the consumer, who has to fight various diseases, food made.

The most common are:
- Obesity
- Insulin resistance
- Hypertension
- Fat metabolism disorders

The reasons for this are the classics: Poor nutrition and little exercise.
The diseases increase the risk of artery calcification, cardiovascular disease and also heart attack or stroke.

In order to change this, a change in diet is necessary. When a healthy diet is combined with exercise, you achieve even better results.

An extensive study by the Institute of European Food Studies found that the principles of a healthy diet are well known to most consumers, but that practical implementation is encountering difficulties for many people.

Despite all the information, the relationship between energy consumption and body usage of energy does not seem to be sufficiently aware. A key factor for many health problems is a long-term unbalanced energy balance with the consequence of obesity. Modern living conditions have led to a huge reduction in physical activity in recent years. As energy intake has not adapted to this development, many have an imbalance between energy intake and consumption.

On one hand, the energy requirement of the body, which can hardly be influenced, is lower for some individuals. This may be due to the basal metabolic rate, which studies say can be smaller when you are overweight than in lean people. This appears to be genetically determined. Women and the elderly have a lower basal metabolic rate than men and young people.

In addition, thermogenesis is also lower when burning food. This means that energy and energy consumed by digestion to generate heat is lower than in lean people. On the other hand, the energy consumption of the body (burning calories) is too low.

Physical activity can increase energy demand. The basal metabolic rate is raised slightly in this way, as there is more muscle. In addition, the intensity of the activities can lead to a high level of additional energy consumption.

By movement, more energy can be consumed and thus a balance to absorb energy can be achieved.
The main problem, however, is overeating. It does not matter whether it is a diet that is too high in carbohydrates or too high in fat. The problem occurs when you eat more calories than your body needs.

Low carb helps you change your lifestyle and restore your body to healthy wellbeing.
Do not wait until you fall ill, but start doing something for your health beforehand!

Consequences of obesity

The number of overweight people in the US is steadily increasing. Not only is the number of overweight people increasing, but so is the level of obesity. From obesity, one speaks from a body measure index (BMI) about 25. From a BMI of more than 30, it is referred to as obesity. The BMI is calculated by body weight divided into kilograms by the length of the body in meters to the square.

The consequences of being overweight are little known. Every year, thousands of people die as a result of being overweight. For people with a BMI of 35, the risk of mortality is twice as high as compared to normal heavyweight. If it is very severe obesity, life expectancy can be reduced by as much as 20 years. Of course, not every kilo has too much the same effect that it leads to a range of subsequent diseases. Just a few kilos too much on the hips are even better for the body than underweight, according to studies.

Similarly, obesity also brings a physical strain. Exhaustion, breathlessness and sweating occur more quickly. This, of course, ends in a vicious circle, since the resulting lack of exercise does not exactly counteract obesity. Obese people have a significantly increased risk of developing cardiovascular disease and ultimately dying from it. Due to the higher body weight, the heart has to work more to supply the entire body with sufficient blood. Due to the increased cardiac load, a heart weakness usually develops in the long run, in which the heart is no longer able to supply the body with blood very well.

Due to the increased fat content, they usually also suffer from an artery calcification, which leads to a narrowing of vessels, so that the body can be less well supplied with blood.

An almost inevitable disease in obese is sugar disease, diabetes mellitus type 2. Due to the increased intake of carbohydrates and sugars, the pancreas produces more insulin, which is supposed to naturally lower the sugar level. Due to the constantly elevated insulin levels, the body eventually forms a resistance to the hormone. This means that the cells no longer react to the hormone. This condition is achieved much earlier in obese people than in people with normal weight.

Increased blood pressure also puts a lot of strain on obese people, which can attack the cardiovascular system. This should definitely be reduced by medication and, above all, by lifestyle changes. In the case of obese people, more water remains and more salts remain in the body so that there is an increased fluid volume in the blood vessels and causes high blood pressure. High blood pressure can have a lasting harmful effect on the eyes and kidneys.

If all the above-mentioned diseases, i.e. sugar disease, fat metabolism disorder and high blood pressure, occur together with obesity, this is called metabolic syndrome. All these diseases also contribute to the development of the artery calcification already mentioned. The risk of a heart attack, as well as a stroke, increases significantly.

In most cases, a fatty liver can develop through a diet that is usually very high in fat. A fatty liver can cause other diseases of the liver, such as inflammation. In some cases, a fatty liver can also develop cirrhosis of the liver, which is associated with an increased risk of cancer and in which the work of the liver is restricted. Likewise, the concentration of uric acid due to the malnutrition of obese is often increased, so that there may be gout attacks.

So-called sleep apnea syndrome is also above-average in obese people. These are short breathing dropouts while sleeping. Mostly the diseased itself won't notice this. It is mostly the partner who will notice this, as, for example, snoring briefly suspends. Due to the respiratory expression, the oxygen content of the blood decreases. The respiratory dropouts put the body under stress, causing blood pressure, pulse and blood sugar to increase. Those affected by sleep apnea syndrome are often tired during the day because the sleep at night is not restful. Sleep apnea syndrome is more common in obese people, as there are more fat pads in the throat area that can close the throat space when inhaled.

The risk of certain cancers is also increased. These include breast cancer and cervical cancer in women. This is due, among other things, to the altered hormone levels of obese women. But also the risk of colorectal cancer and gallbladder cancer is elevated in both men and women.

Of course, the increased body weight also puts more strain on the joints, so that wear and tear occur more quickly. Often, the increased joint load will be accompanied by malpositions of the legs or even feet and malpositions of the body. The knee, hip and ankle joints, as well as the spine, are mainly affected.

Virtually any of the listed consequences can be reduced by a weight reduction or the severity of the disease that has occurred can be minimized. Life expectancy is also rising again after a successful weight loss.

With proper nutrition combined with exercise, it is possible to pre-emptively address these diseases. It is also possible to improve if you change your diet, even though you have already fallen ill.

Many people underestimate the risk of consequential diseases of obesity. However, these are very serious since they can become life-threatening!

Voracious Appetite
(Munchies, Cravings attacks)

To have the munchies or a voracious appetite describe the rampant craving for sweet, salty or fatty food.

Our body actually wants to show us that it lacks vital nutrients. However, cravings are not only a symptom of nutrient deficiencies but also of physical and mental illnesses or hormonal changes such as diabetes mellitus, bulimia diseases or even during pregnancy.

Cravings are a form of hunger that can only be poorly maintained. While normal hunger can sometimes be endured, cravings are usually not to be tamed. Sometimes cravings can be vital, for example, if you haven't eaten anything for a long time or you've been very active in sports.
Regular cravings, however, may as well be the symptom of serious physical or psychological illness. Those who are hungry and are constantly plagued by voracious hunger may suffer from a metabolic disease such as diabetes mellitus or hyperthyroidism.

The emergence of the feeling of hunger is a complicated process, which is regulated via various messengers and receptors of the body. In addition, behaviour, sensory perceptions and habits control the feeling of hunger. All information converges mainly in the hypothalamus and in the brain stem. The brain's job is then to control the balance between energy consumption and food intake.

Some people, however, are constantly hungry-with them, regulation is disrupted. Then there might appear diseases such as obesity or bulimia, to name a few. Both diseases are known for hunger attacks and a purely psychological ongoing feeling of hunger.

Blood sugar (glucose) also plays an important role in the context of hunger. Glucose is the most important source of energy in our body, whose task is to convert immediately into energy or is initially stored in cells with the help of insulin. The less glucose in the blood, the faster the cravings and thus the eating attacks.

As you learned in the previous chapter, some carbohydrate-rich foods take longer to break down into their constituents, which causes glucose to stay in the blood longer. This causes you to be full for longer and munchies/cravings/hunger attacks can be avoided. This can be achieved, for example, with wholemeal bread or legumes or nuts.

But what exactly are the causes of cravings?
There are many different causes for cravings. In addition to physical and psychological causes such as diabetes mellitus, hyperfunction of the thyroid gland, metabolic diseases, obesity or bulimia, other causes may include:

- Stress
- Medicines (psychopharmaceuticals)
- Diets
- Migraine
- Worm infections
- Alcohol dependence
- boredom
- Long dining breaks
- Sleep deprivation
- Habits
- Cannabis use
- Too many quick carbs/sugar
- Too many sweets

As you can see, there are various causes that can trigger munchie attacks. The habit is one of them, too. Chocolate makes you feel good, many of you might know this feeling. If you get used to the bar of chocolate in the evening on the couch, you may constantly have cravings for it when you lie on the couch. Or if you are bored, you might just get up get some snacks from the kitchen.

You see, a bad habit can lead to very bad eating behaviour, which brings your body out of balance.

If you suffer from regular munchie attacks, these tips may help you to prevent cravings:

1. Take time for food! The body can thus develop a feeling of satiety.
2. Don't eat in front of the TV.
3. Set regular meal times and try to avoid unplanned snacks! If you absolutely need something for in between, you prefer to grab fruit than a chocolate bar.
4. Avoid stress! But also avoid boredom!
5. Don't get your body used to sins! Be sure to need your piece of chocolate, eat it right after the main course.
6. Try and stuff your belly with healthy foods, greens, veggies until you are full. Don't use pasta or bread as the filling part.
7. Avoid making it a habit to eat sweets or salty as a reward for something.

If you follow this advice, you can manage to escape the cravings.

Chapter 3: Different Low Carb Diets

There are various nutritional theories that make it possible to customize low carb individually. Depending on the method, carbohydrates are reduced very drastically or rather slowly.

However, each method has the same basic principle:

Avoid highly carbohydrate-rich foods!

Low carb relies on protein-rich foods such as eggs, milk, fish or meat and allows you to cook the right low carb dish for every taste.

Especially at the beginning, it is very important to deal with the different theories in order to find the right thing for you personally.

What nutritional theories are there?

The Logi Theory

Logi stands for "low glycemic and insulinemic," meaning "low insulin – and blood sugar levels." The main feature of this method is to maintain a low blood sugar effect.

This avoids blood sugar fluctuations and insulin levels also remain uniformly low. This prevents excessive calorie storage and thus bring many health benefits.

Imagine a pyramid. At the bottom, you will find low-starch vegetables and also fruit, which is the basis of the Logi diet. Low-starch because starch is a sugar. Vegetables and salad can be eaten abundantly, provided you use the fibre rich and low in starch products. These include avocado, cabbage, zucchini or leaf salad or radishes.

These saturate best and affect metabolism in a positive way. Even with some fruit, you could choose different types of berries or citrus fruits. Caution with very sweet fruits, they could contain a greater amount of sugar and carbohydrates. Only eat these in season and in small portions.

The Logi method makes a "5 a day" recommendation. Three portions of vegetables and two portions of fruit should be consumed daily.

The basic ingredients should then be extended. Dairy products and also low-fat fish or low-fat meat are in the pyramid above the fruit and vegetables. These foods should often be eaten as basic food.

A level above dairy and low-fat fish and meat you will now find the products you should eat less. These include white rice, pasta, sweetened cereals or bread rolls and bread.

At the top of the Logi Pyramid, you will find the foods that you should rarely or not eat at all. These are pies, chips, sugary drinks and sweets.

Always keep this pyramid in mind and you will see how easy it is to avoid the top 2 layers.
Low Carb offers many varied and healthy ways to eat healthily.

Also, with this method, you don't have to be afraid of the well-known yo-yo effect. The LOGI diet fully meets the needs of metabolism, as the organism receives all the necessary vital substances and can thus work with full power.

Munchie attacks and stress eating will no longer be in your way from losing weight.

The Atkins Diet

The Atkins diet is named after inventor Robert Atkins and initially drastically reduces the intake of carbohydrates. It uses fat and proteins as the main energy source.

During the first 14 days, you should not consume more than 20 grams of carbohydrates daily. According to Atkins, soy products, meat and eggs provide the perfect combination of amino acids to help burn fat cells. Bread is strictly forbidden here.

Due to the very small amount of carbohydrates that can be absorbed, the body is forced to immediately go to the fat reserves and get the energy it needs. After 14 days, more and more nutrient-rich carbohydrates can now be consumed. These can be found in nuts, seeds, vegetables, berries, and also legumes. 5 grams more should be consumed each week.

If you realize that weight loss stops, reduce the intake by 5 grams again. This value shows you how many carbohydrates you can consume and still lose weight. The carbohydrate intake should be between 40 and 60 grams.

Following this phase, the weight decrease should slowly come to a standstill. Once the targeted weight has been reached, the choice of permitted products increases enormously. Atkins recommends plenty of fish, vegetables and fruit. Potatoes or pasta should rather be an exception or disappear completely from the meal plan. This final phase is intended to be the permanent further form of nutrition.

The Low Carb High Fat Method

Low Carb High Fat means little carbohydrates – many healthy fats. This diet comes from Sweden and is particularly convincing about the health aspects. Diabetes is positively affected, skin diseases disappear and stomach intestinal problems are a thing of the past.

The food allowed includes regional and seasonal products. The food should be unprocessed and freshly prepared.

Eggs, fish and seafood, meat, poultry, salads, vegetables and fats and oils are included on the menu. Drinks include unsweetened teas, water or coffee.

Carbohydrate-rich vegetables such as potatoes or root vegetables, cereal products such as rice, pasta or bread, charcuterie and margarine must be avoided. With drinks, you should definitely do without juices, soft drinks and also beer, wheat beer, liqueurs, etc.!

This reduces the carbohydrate content leads to a steadfast low blood sugar level and thus also to a low insulin emission so that the fat burning has a free run.

The Ketogenic Diet

The ketogenic diet is currently probably the strictest low carb variant, which demands an extremely high level of discipline and knowledge. So not exactly suitable for beginners.

It is carbohydrate limited, protein and energy accounted for and a very high-fat form of diet that mimics the metabolism of hunger. This diet leads the body to no longer obtain the energy requirements from fat and glucose, but only from fat and glucose replacement, which is called ketone bodies.

In the case of a ketogenic diet, the energy requirement (about 80 – 320 kJ/kg) and the protein requirement (0.7 – 2 gram/kg) are calculated, resulting in the ketogenic ratio. This ratio determines the weight ratio of fat to carbohydrates and proteins. For example, a ketogenic ratio of 4:1 means that meals must be 80% fat. The remaining 20% are proteins. Therefore, you can only eat a small amount of carbohydrates to maintain useful and effective ketosis.

This diet requires careful calculation and determination, which is why it is important to perform it with the help of a doctor. The appropriate implementation of this conversion must be monitored regularly via urine or blood ketoses (similar to diabetics). Nevertheless, this can also be done without monitoring and cooperation with doctors, but this form of nutrition is not yet recommended for beginners, as it is very complex.

For me personally, the ketogenic diet would not be my long term nutrition option because I know good, healthy carbs are important for my brain, body and wellbeing.
This is a reminder that what works for you or me might not work for others. I am a vegetarian and eat dairy free, so yes I do need other healthy natural carbs (potatoes, oats, lentils, chickpeas, etc.) to get enough energy and vital nutrients...

These four nutritional theories are basic ideas that can help you start with low carb.

All four theories are based on these principles:

- Little carbohydrates, healthy fats.
- Strenuous diets that only briefly lead to success are a thing of the past and Low Carb will inspire you in the future.
- It keeps you fit, slim and, above all, healthy and is customizable. You don't

have to focus on just one product, with which you lose weight quickly, but can eat delicious, healthy meals and still lose weight.

If you start with one of the above low-carb dietary changes, you naturally have expectations, goals and desires for the new form of nutrition. What is realistic? How many pounds can you lose in what time? All these questions are sure to buzz through your mind at the start of the low-carb changeover.

It should not be forgotten, however, that every person reacts differently to the dietary change. Every human body is different. One loses disturbing fat faster, the other slower. You and your body have your own pace and that's a good thing too! Some people need more carbs than other people, so if you feel too tired and have a lack of power after some weeks of eating low carb, think about adding some healthy carbs like potatoes, etc to your meals.
Therefore, be sure to avoid comparing yourself to others.

How many pounds you will lose in the first few months after the diet change depends, among other things, on how overweight you were at the start of low carb. The higher the starting weight, the more weight you will lose in the beginning. Many low-carb people report 1-2 kilos and more per week.

Don't be frustrated if the weight doesn't go down that fast after about one to two months. It's normal for it to stagnate. The reason for this is the slowing metabolism. Even if you don't see any success for a short time, stay tuned! It would be fatal to stop just then! After this frustrating time, the sun will soon emerge from behind the clouds. Weight loss will continue continuously thereafter. It is helpful to exercise more and more during this time. In this way, successes can be made visible again more quickly!

Thousands of people have already been inspired by low carb. Try it too.

Chapter 4: The path to the changeover begins in your mind

Oftentimes when we hear the word "diet" we think directly of renunciation and cravings. Refusing means limitation and afflicts the mindset very negatively.

In order to be able to change your diet, it is therefore important to detach yourself from negative thoughts.

Low carb does not mean giving up on food, but to try new foods, and eat things in the future that do your health and your body good.

A big advantage of the low-carb diet is that you can prepare almost all known and favourite dishes low-carb style and therefore only have to change and not give up. With constant restrictions, the fun and enjoyment of food can be lost and the change in diet will never end successfully.

First, start erasing negative ways of thinking from your mind and building positive ones. Try exercise to build your self-confidence.

Some people stand in front of a mirror and say to themselves, "I look great, I can do this!"

You should store positive thoughts about it in your head and keep saying to yourself "That's delicious and healthy!" Or "Today I cook a menu which I like and which is still healthy!" Positive ways of thinking promote motivation and help you stay tuned.

If you're constantly persuading yourself "I need to eat the food because it's healthy, even if it doesn't taste" this is the wrong approach. The motivation is quickly lost and quickly you end up eating again at the tried and tested, which was originally responsible for the overweight.

Positive basic settings help you stay focused, even if the inner demons try to drag you to the "nasty" side of the diet again and again....

Positive thinking is a powerful tool that helps us to live a life that we are dreaming of.
The only thing we have to do is use it properly and keep working on it all the time. At some point, it becomes a habit and we manage to always allow positive thoughts.

Of course, it takes a while, but it's doable. The first thing to do is to set a goal. First, focus on what you want to achieve and WHY! Then build your positive thoughts on top and consider how you want to achieve this goal. Split it into small doable steps. You will see that a positive way of thinking makes everything a lot easier for you!

However, we must not forget the other side either. Even the negative ways of thinking can be very powerful! Even if you try to dislodge them, they may return unconsciously. How? By going back through unpleasant experiences, mistakes, embarrassing moments or even wrong decisions.

Self-awareness is easily scratched and negative thoughts like "I can't do this" or "I'm way too disorganised" quickly take back the control of our brains.

Negative events are firmly dug into the subconscious and quickly come out again when you experience similar things. This is hard to control. Nevertheless, one should always try to let these experiences rest and always keep in mind, even in case of failure, "I am good the way I am! I can do this better and I will succeed!" With this positive basic attitude, you can strongly influence the negative ways of thinking and that is exactly what the point of the matter is.

A dietary change can only succeed if you know perfectly well, "I want that! I like that! I'm living healthier from now on!"
Don't be guided by negative thoughts! Take advantage of the good thoughts and you will notice how easy it is to be proud of yourself!

6 Important Low Carb Principles

#1 Low carb doesn't mean "no carb"

It is never healthy to avoid certain natural nutrition completely. The body needs carbohydrates, but the right ones! Never give up on them completely. Carbohydrates provide energy to your body and the brain also relies on it. Just eat the "good" carbohydrates.

#2 Always be aware of dinner

"Eat breakfast like a king, lunch like a prince and dinner like a beggar", who doesn't know the saying? There's some truth to it! Carbohydrates should be represented at breakfast and lunch. At dinner, you should do without it or at least be less than 20 grams per serving. Nightly fat burning is otherwise significantly lowered and success is limited.

#3 Eat lots of vegetables and salad

Of course, you know that vegetables and salad serve as the basis for the low-carb diet. Still, even before the dietary change, you start to

slowly get your body used to the fact that these are now your main components.
With these small steps, you learn to get used to the changeover slowly.

#4 Drink enough – But also the right thing

Unsweetened teas or water should be on your table every day. Sugary soft drinks, juices or beer are not part of the low-carb diet and should only be absolute exceptions or banned from the refrigerator altogether.

#5 Consume plenty of protein

30-35% of your daily diet should be protein. These can be found in dairy products, eggs, lentils, chickpeas, nutritional yeast and also in fish and meat. Sufficient proteins promote weight loss enormously.

#6 Eat healthy fats

Healthy fats don't make you fat. They serve as energy sources and are therefore indispensable. High-fat products such as nuts, fish, seeds, olive oil or avocado must therefore not be missing on any meal plan!

The metabolism of our body will take a while to switch to the low-carbohydrate diet.

Initially, you will notice that you lose weight faster in the beginning than a short time in. This is because the body initially loses water in the beginning. Don't let this realization take away your courage and stay tuned. After losing water, the body will resort to the fat reserves and the pounds you will lose then will also disappear permanently.

This requires patience and discipline. Don't be seduced by the "nasty" carbohydrates and grab the next best snack because you're frustrated.
Stick to these 6 principles and your dietary change will be permanently and you will see success soon.

Escaping the insulin roller coaster...

Low carb nutrition works so well because you keep the insulin in check. Insulin levels slowly make it settle in and work together with blood sugar levels. Low carb supports the healthy release of insulin and prevents getting into the roller coaster that combines insulin and cravings. If too much sugar and carbohydrates enter the human body, insulin is released more and more, which transports the sugar into the cells and then leaves no room for healthy nutrients. The fat cells grow, the body reacts and cravings/hunger attacks follow. Get out of this roller coaster now!

Don't let your cells become clogged with the unnecessary fat maker, but carry the nutrients through the low carb nutrition to where they belong, so your body doesn't fill the fat cells, but use the fat to provide you with important energies!

3 supportive rules to follow

Rule # 1:
Between each meal, there should be a 4-5 hour break so that blood sugar levels have time to return to normal.

Rule #2:
Drink plenty of water! Abundant water helps to flood toxins out of cells and protects against headaches and circulatory problems when blood pressure should drop. Sometimes the hunger feeling in your stomach is actually just thirst. So drink a glass of water first. If you are still hungry afterwards eat something, if not, you were only thirsty.

Rule #3:
Move! By exercise, the basal metabolic rate of energy increases and more calories can be burned.

Avoid the insulin worsening your physical well-being and restrict your intake of carbohydrates. This is the only way you can escape from the insulin roller coaster and clear the way for healthy and helpful nutrients.

Overcoming the 3 most common problems

According to a survey from dietdoctor with 1,400 participants, three of the most common problems where:

Problem #1: Slow Weight Loss
Problem #2: Carb cravings
Problem #3: Low Energy

Additionally, when it comes to a change in nutrition with the goal of weight loss, there are 3 common problems most of us face.

Problem #1: Slow Weight Loss
Problem #2: Carb cravings
Problem #3: Low Energy

So let's see what this all about and what we can do to solve these problems.

Problem #1: Slow Weight Loss

When it comes to sustainable weight loss, it is actually recommended to lose weight slowly. The typical recommendation is a weight loss of one to two pounds a week.

This might sound very slow for someone who badly likes to lose weight, but it is actually known that if you lose weight slowly, it is more likely to help you to maintain the weight loss for the long term.

You should know that 1 pound of fat (0.45 kilogram) contains 3,500 calories. This means you need to burn 500 more calories than you eat each day to lose 1 pound. 500 calories x 7 days are 3.500 calories.

If you lose weight very quickly you actually might not lose a lot of fat actually. Quick weight loss is mostly a loss of water and even lean tissue since it is very hard for your body to burn that much fat during a short period.

So remember when you are starting to become impatient, it is normal to lose weight slowly and it might be even the better and more sustainable way if you like to lose weight for the long term. And that's what we all want right?

It is also normal to lose weight faster during the first weeks and then you might face a plateau where you feel like you don't lose any weight anymore. During this phase, try and implement a bit more exercise, try to check your food, maybe you got some foods into your daily meal plan that you could change for a short period, to see if they were the reason your weight loss stagnated.

And don't lose patience. The extra pounds on your body didn't appear overnight, so they won't disappear overnight either. Keep on track, keep moving, don't get frustrated, but keep on going. You'll see you will overcome the plateau and lose the next extra pounds soon.

Problem#2: Carb Cravings

I'll promise you they will come. And they sometimes hit hard. Carb Cravings... Our body is used to sugar, it also needs sugar, but mostly we just eat too much of it, so your body will crave more sugar quickly.

Sweet is actually the first taste humans get from mothers milk. It is our prefered taste from the beginning.

Carbs stimulate the release of the feel-good brain chemical serotonin.

Sugar is not only the favourite taste for most of us, it is also known to release endorphins that calm and relax us and it can even cause a natural high. The problem is just that we eat too much of it. So our body is kind of addicted to sugar after a while of over-consuming sugar. The recommended sugar portion would be about 6 tsp for women and 9 for men per day. An average American actually consumes 22 teaspoons of added sugar a day!

So just be aware that those carb cravings will overcome you at the beginning of the nutritional shift. Because your body needs to get used to less sugar.

So how to get rid of those cravings? Eat less sugar.
When we started our Low Carb journey my dad told me to start with a green week. Sound relaxing but was no fun! The green week potentially allows eating green food only. Green veggies have less to almost no sugar. So we went cold turkey and yeah we had a lot of fights during this week :D But I can tell you the craving for sugar was gone after this week. And then just don't start eating lots of sugar again. This is the thing, the more sugar you

eat the more you crave, the less sugar you eat, the less sugar your body will crave.

In case you really need a sweet fix find healthier snacks. Like:

- Get a banana with peanut butter.
- Eat a piece of dark chocolate (the more cocoa the better, and look for less sweetened too).
- Grab some nuts and dried fruit.
  Get some fresh fruits, e.g. berries.
- Get out and do something.

Often we crave sugary foods and drinks when we feel bored, so go for a walk, bike ride, do some exercise, etc.

Try to avoid the whole day snacking. Keep 4-5 hours between your meals, then eat as much until you really feel full and satisfied. Don't eat some snacks every hour, that will actually keep your body crave more than if you "fast" 4-5 hours between your meals.

It is like when you start to drink tap water only after you've been drinking only sweet drinks for many years. In the beginning, you will be like Ewwww disgusting! After a while, you will feel like that about the sweet drinks, not the unsweetened drinks.

Problem #3: Lack of Energy

If you change your nutrition to Low Carb it can happen that you feel a lack of energy after a while. We actually experienced that too. We ate a little bit stricter Low Carb during the first few months, and after a while both of us felt really tired, had no real energy, running was very hard....

That's when I researched and read a lot about how different people bodies react on Low Carb, and that it is totally normal that some people need a little more carbs than other people. And since we are eating strict vegetarian and I eat dairy free, we didn't have all the fat etc from meat and dairy so we added some natural carbs into our diet and energy came back asap.

So since we reached our weight goals, we added some carbs, grains, cereals to our regular diet. We eat oats with fruits in the morning, when I bake bread I use spelt flour or buckwheat. We don't restrict any veggies or fruits, but we don't eat heaps of fruits. It is important to find your own powerfoods. Find your own natural carbs you like to include to your diet. Don't listen to anybody else. Our bodies react differently, so if your best friends tells you not to eat bananas because of the carbs, but you feel much better if you eat a banana in the morning and you don't see your weight gaining, stick to it!

Overcoming the 3 biggest fears

Fear #1: Giving up foods I love

Who said you have to? Don't give up some of the foods you love. But yes for sure, eat less and in moderation if they are full of calories and sugar and trans fats.

If your favourite food is a double burger with double cheese or the biggest chocolate bar with heaps of caramel and sweetened milk chocolate, don't eat them regularly! Eat them in moderation, once a month. Or when you reached your mid-term goal of weight loss.

Your favourite food is bread? Try different kinds of bread. Try a different kind of flour. Try and make a lower carb bread. And don't eat bread 3 times a day. Reduce it to once a day, or every second day.

And always look for new favourite foods.

Maybe you can find a healthier alternative that could happen to become your new favourite snack? Like a self-made vegan dip from sunflower seeds and dried tomatoes? Or the potato peel chips you can make quickly in your oven when you are craving some snacks.

What I love about researching food and recipes is that I always discover new recipes or even veggies I never tried before and I now love.

Fear #2: Eating lots of fat

When you hear about Low Carb people tell you you need to eat more protein and fat, and then you remember: Wait didn't they say that fat is unhealthy and makes you actually fat?

I can understand, I thought like that when I was younger too. Why? Because advertising tells you: eat low fat products to lose weight.

Did you know most low fat products can actually be more calorie dense and have more carbs? The trick is that fat is very good for the taste of food. So to make convenience low fat food tasty for humans, they need something else.. if they can't take fat, what do they take? Sugar, sugar substitutes. All of those refined stuff that make our bodies crave even more. A statistic of npr.org say that people got fatter since they called out on fat in the 80ties.

The right fat doesn't make you fat. I am talking more about fat in an extra chapter. If you eat heaps of the wrong fat that could make you sick and overweight. But focus on good and healthy fats from nuts, avocados, rapeseed oil, linseed oil, olive oil, coconut oil, organic, grass-fed cheese, etc. and you are ok. Stay away from solid trans fats. These are highly processed to stay solid in warmer temperature and are used in too many convenience products and are not very healthy.

The only solid fat that is ok to eat is coconut oil. It will be liquid and transparent above 72 degrees F and get solid under 70 degrees F.

We need to understand that real natural foods are not the enemies. So don't be afraid of natural unprocessed food.

The convenience highly processed foods are those we should be careful with!
From everything else you can eat a little bit of everything. A good mix of healthy natural food would be the best.

Fear #3: Fear of Failing

Everytime we set goals for ourselves and talk about them we are afraid to fail. But what would actually happen if we fail? Nothing much mostly. If you don't lose all the weight during the amount of time you hoped, there won't happen anything other than you continue.
Real friends won't laugh at you or call you a loser. It is mostly ourselves that would judge us more than others would do.

What helps here would be to set smaller goals. Goals you can achieve easier. And if you then might lose some weight quicker you'll feel much better.

I like to compare that with running a marathon. Nobody would try to do that after a week or after a month of training. You would fail for sure.

But setting realistic goals, like training for 6 months, or if you haven't been running at all a 9 months training plan, yes there is a great chance you will succeed and finish the marathon with a smile.

So by setting realistic goals, getting support from family and friends who could maybe even push you on weak days, there will be only success in sight, no failure.

Exercise and Low Carb
The Perfect Combination

Exercising will support you in addition to your low carb meal plan to visibly lose fat pads.

Exercise consumes energies and especially calories, which can then no longer be converted into body fat. The decreased carbohydrate increase means that you automatically consume only as many calories as you need to be full. If you move more and more, the body is forced to use fat reserves after a very short time in order to get the energy that the muscles demand.

Exercise doesn't mean you have to do competitive sports. It could be enough if, for example, instead of the car, you take the bike or walk. Consider which paths to master on foot. Maybe the nearest supermarket is just around the corner,

Or the child's school just a few streets away. Then leave your car at home and walk!

You can also use a bicycle as an alternative. Cycling stimulates many different muscle groups in the body and consumes energy. On the bike, you can enjoy the fresh air and at the same time do something for your body. In most cases, you can even get to your destination faster than by car. The annoying professional traffic and search for a parking space would be a thing of the past.

It is also easy to implement movement in everyday life. Ignore elevators and escalators. Take the stairs and walk the few steps. Your body will thank you.

Even at home, it is possible to move without exercising directly. Get involved in playing with your children or dog. Play catch, frisbee or even ball games. Of course, ordinary sports are also perfect. Jogging, walking or swimming and dancing are useful supplements to the low carb diet. Move at least three times a week and be active. You will certainly find something that suits you!

After just two weeks, you will notice that your body is already tightening. This is because the muscles grow through movement. This has not only an external effect but also an inner one. Muscle cells consume more energy than fat cells even at rest.

And then you'll have achieved what we all dream of:

Your body now consumes energy even if you rest and that, if you continue to feed low carb, will, over time, make you lose pounds faster.

We usually "collect" the extra pounds because we sit too much, are concerned or frightened and that causes stress. Stress causes us to stuff everything into ourselves to forget our worries. Unfortunately, this does not make us forget our worries, but only builds up fat pads, which cause us further worries.

Against stress and stress-eating helps exercise. Muscle work helps to relieve stress and, above all, also makes us feel good, as exercise releases happiness hormones. Those who are on the move have little time to think and at the same time do a lot of good for their body.

Many people find it difficult to do exercise on their own. You are tired, have no desire or the inner demon is usually stronger. What helps is to find a motivational partner! Face the new task as a couple or maybe triple or join a class. Plan your exercises together, so that there is a commitment to actually do them.

Keep in mind that your training partner should be on an equal level with you. This means he doesn't run away from you when it goes into the field for jogging. This could lead very quickly to frustration and quitting.

Try to take a class at a gym that needs to be paid for. Many people attend classes more regularly because they are more valuable. After all, they paid for it, so they go too!

Outsmart your inner demon and put on your activewear. Exercise in combination with low carb is the best combination in the fight against annoying pounds.
When I started to run regularly again I couldn't believe how much better my mind and body felt and I lost pounds even quicker.

Chapter 5 Let's go!

First steps into your low carb life...

You don't need a holiday or a lot of time to change your diet to Low Carb. The only thing you need is the thought: "I want to change my lifestyle!"
You should also think in advance about which method of low carb nutrition is suitable for you.

In Chapter 2 you got to know various dietary methods that either slowly reduced carbohydrates or drastically reduced carbohydrates. Think about what exactly you want to achieve and set small goals.

Start today to let the thought about low carb work in your mind and imagine how you will live from tomorrow quite carefree and slightly lower in carbohydrates.

Now let the action do the talking. Walk into the kitchen, grab a box and browse your cupboards in search of carbohydrate-rich foods. Banish these either forever, or for a set time. However, let them disappear from your kitchen so you have no reason to fall back on it.

But what belongs into the box?

Definitely all the sweets! Only chocolate with at least 70% cocoa content and low sugar is allowed to stay in the cupboard.
Also, all chips, salty and sweet bars and all nibbles need to go, except natural nuts! You can keep them and nibble pure or use them to refine salads or hot dishes.

Likewise, the bread must disappear. Only Flaxseed crisp-bread is recommended because it has little carbohydrates.

White wheat noodles, white rice, potatoes and sugar also belong in the box. Fill up your cupboard with whole grains or soy. This is low in carbohydrates and may be on the low carb meal plan.

Convenience foods like sauces, ready-made salad sauces and ketchup & Co. also belong in the box, they are full of sugar or sugar additives.

Banish alcoholic beverages, especially beer, soft drinks and fruit juices from your fridge.

From now on you will drink water and unsweetened teas.

Wheat flour also has nothing to do in your kitchen as of now. From now on, use soy flour, linseed or almond flour, coconut flour.

The day before you change to low carb, you should write a list showing all the foods that will be included on your meal plan in the future. Various vegetables and fruits are also on this list, and also nuts. It also makes sense to have some canned food (chickpeas, olives) as well as fish (seabream, salmon, make sure they are sustainably caught!) and some frozen stuff such as vegetables (spinach, vegetable mixes, broccoli) and fruits (berry mix, raspberries, strawberries).

This serves as a stock for at home, so that you have a lot of healthy foods you can choose from if you get overwhelmed by sudden cravings, during the first days/weeks of your low carb journey.

To avoid making it even harder, it's helpful to avoid certain aisles, such as the chips and chocolate aisles, in the supermarket. ;-)

If you avoid plastic packaged food, you will not only do something good for the environment (91% of plastic that is produced worldwide is not getting recycled), but you will also avoid a lot of unhealthy food. So try and challenge yourself to quit/reduce the amount of plastic wrapped food and you will see how positive your grocery shopping will affect your weight and wellbeing.

Almost done...

Now all that's missing is a perfect organization. Make yourself a weekly plan. Don't forget to plan meals and take enough time to do so. You should also plan some exercise units so that you can reach your desired weight and a successful diet change faster.
Organizing your day avoids stress and without stress, fewer hunger attacks appear!
Plan your day/week and you'll see you are perfectly equipped to start a low carb life with healthy well-being!

Changing doesn't mean sacrifice

Low carb is not a diet where you have to go without everything you loved to eat.

Low carb is a dietary change that changes eating patterns but which does not mean renunciation.

Any carbohydrate-rich ingredient or product can be replaced by a low carb ingredient/product. You can find a lot of alternative recipes and certain convenience low carb products such as Shirataki noodles or low carb pizza, so you don't have to do without pizza, bread and co. However, with convenience products, make sure they are not full of unhealthy fat. Always read the labels!!

At first, it is advisable to pay more attention to carbohydrates. The diet should be low in carbohydrates and balanced to achieve faster customer success. If you reached your targeted weight, it is possible to eat carbohydrate-richer foods again in between, but only in moderation and not daily.

So if you're feeding on low carb, it's not a sacrifice, it's just a change. Change usually brings us success and are important goals in a person's life. Don't be afraid to make a difference. Because only if you try it you can see how valuable this change is to your life and, above all, to your health!

Just remember: never give up carbohydrates completely! Carbohydrates are vital to survival and control important functions in a person's body.

Low Carb in the Supermarket

Off to the supermarket – These basics belong in the shopping carts

You are now prepared, finished your shopping list, got your reusable shopping bags and now you are on your way to the supermarket.

But what exactly are the basics that every low-carb person should have in their kitchen?

- Fish and seafood (Tip: always look out for sustainably caught fish(MSC))
- Low-fat meat (Tip: always look for grass fed/local/organic)
- Fresh, regional and seasonal vegetables and fruit (maybe even plastic free)
- Berries (fresh or frozen)
- Lemons
- Organic eggs
- Raw cheese – or milk (grass-fed, organic)
- High-quality fats
- Butter (organic)
- Joghurt (organic, grass-fed)
- High-quality olive oil, avocado oil, linseed oil

- Nuts and almonds (maybe you can find them in bulk and bring your reusable bulk bags)
- fruits (berries or citrus fruits are best)
- Spices
- Fresh herbs
- Uniodized salt
- Coconut and almond flour
- Cocoa powder (unsweetened)
- Chocolate with at least 70% cocoa content and low sugar
- Sugar substitutes for desserts (e.g. stevia, xylitol)
- Crispbread
- Water (Tap water is safe to drink in many cities. Will save you money and plastic bottles. Get a purifier if you want)
- Unsweetened teas

These are the basics that are enough for a successful start to a low-carb life.

In addition to the food, there are also helpful kitchen utensils for processing the food, which should not be missing in any household. These include:

- Silicone baking moulds of any kind
- Blender for larger quantities of vegetables, fruits and herbs

- Nut grate (if grated they can be processed better)
- Coffee mill (for sesame, flaxseed ...)
- Spiral cutters for vegetable noodles (zoodles)

Eating low carb sounds more complicated than it is. In principle, you eat the same thing, only with other ingredients. And as always it will just take a short time of getting used to it and then it will become easier and after a while the new norm.

Low-carb foods are only allowed to have a small proportion of carbohydrates. A lot of people think that with the Low Carb Diet also a loss of food choice goes by. In the same way, some people think the taste gets lost.

However, this is not the case...

It is actually the other way around. You will get to know much more foods than before because you think outside the box. There are a number of tasty low carb foods that offer full flavour while meeting the requirements of a low carb food. You might discover some old but new to you seasonal vegetables and fruits from your area.

Low carb foods will provide the body with essential substances, but do not affect weight with empty calories.

They are the ideal alternative to carbohydrate- heavy foods and can be easily implemented.

The conscious diet with selected ingredients is always a bit more elaborate than the fast kitchen from the microwave. However, those who decide to change their diet will soon find that the effort is well worth it and that the far-reaching renunciation of carbohydrates is by no means associated with a renunciation of variety and enjoyment! And if a new habit has evolved it will become normal and does not feel like extra work anymore.

You can find many low carb recipes nowadays. This is how beginners, as well as advanced low-carb eaters, are guaranteed to get enough Ideas and also instructions. From breakfast to dinner, you will find plenty of delicious dishes for all tastes and occasions. Of course, there are no limits to your own creativity either.

Low carb is for everyone. Also for vegetarians and vegans. Also, they should not eat strictly low carb but moderate and use more natural carbs to get all the calories needed.

If you don't want to miss out on cookies and cakes, there are a number of products such as almond or soy flour that are excellent for baking.

The products listed above will help you start your low carbohydrate life and get you on track to do something good for you and your body.

Stay patient and persevere!

Eating out:
What do I need to be aware of?

Everyone knows it, you have a lunch break and go with your colleague out for lunch in the canteen or in a bistro. Or in the evening your partner invites you to a restaurant. What now? If you go out it's not possible to take your own food with you.

Don't worry! Don't be afraid of restaurant visits. Enjoy the food! Especially at work in the canteen you can simply walk past the carbohydrate-rich side dishes and grab the vegetables and the salad bar. Also, use bean seeds to provide you with healthy carbohydrates! Green beans also go well with the low-carb diet, as these are rich in protein.

Be careful with fried vegetable or fish sticks! Sounds low carb at first, but it's not. The dough is mostly made of plenty of potatoes and flour, so hidden carbohydrates lurk!

In the restaurant, you should also disregard the side dishes and look at the menu for the vegetarian dishes. Look for salads with vinegar and oil dressing. Yoghurt dressing has a lot of sugar included mostly.

In most cases, however, bread or baguettes are also served, which you should definitely do without! Rather ask for a larger portion and ask the service to omit the bread. If they serve the bread and you don't eat it they will most likely throw it away. So always remember to order: "No bread please" to avoid food waste.

At dessert, you're not going to get around carbs. Order a sorbet with fresh fruit instead of a cake! Enjoy the food and stop as soon as you're full.
Back home, you can make the "little sin" disappear again through a few stricter low-carb meals.

As you can see, you don't have to do without anything! A small change in food is enough and you can even continue your low carb diet outside the house.

If you find it difficult to make a special order at the restaurant, ask your companion to do it for you. Sometimes you just lack the self-confidence or you don't want to be rude, but there's a simple solution to every problem! And it is definitely not rude to order a salad without the bread.

Enjoy your food and eat consciously all the time!

Practical tips and tricks for eating out of the house

With these little tips and tricks, eating out of the house will be even easier for you! It is always good to be prepared and have a few snacks on you to avoid the quick chocolate bar snack...
We want to start with 10 delicious snacks for in between:

- Nut Mix
- Nuts of all kinds
- Small tomatoes and a hard-boiled egg
- Olives or capers
- Cheese snack (preferably from organic and grass-fed cows)
- Cottage cheese
- Vegetables of any kind
- A slice of low-fat ham with vegetables
- Fruits like berries
- Cold roast chicken

8 tasty lunch box meals

We would also like to introduce you to the tastiest 8 lunch box meals, which are perfect for a lunch break:

Hot soups or stews (bring them in a thermal box, or if you can, reheat in the office kitchen)
- Avocado salad
- Vegan "tuna" salad
- Avocado cream sweet or spicy with veggie sticks
- Italian antipasti
- Chickpeas mixed with some spices and oil (very rich in protein)
- Herring salad
- Homemade tofu, sausage or cheese salad with vegetables

Of course, the visit to the restaurant should not be missing. Here are the best dishes you can choose from the menu:

- Soups with vegetable insert (minestrone, tomato soup, vegetable soup)
- Clear soups with egg
- Antipasti
- Beef carpaccio

- Tartar
- Beef tartare
- Tomato – mozzarella salad
- Various salads (except potato or pasta salad, and cancel the bread)
- Low-fat meat or fish dishes with plenty of vegetables as a side dish Wok dishes, pan dishes without rice

And you can also enjoy the desserts:
- Cheese plate
- Fruit salad
- Small ice cream, sorbet with fresh fruit
- A small portion of Mousse Au Chocolat (best from dark chocolate)

Chapter 6: Low Carb Diet Plan

What does a low-carb diet plan look like?

You alone are the designer of your diet plan to your personal liking! Check out the recipes and pick out what you like.

Nutrition plans should always be structured in such a way that all daily needs are distributed among breakfast, lunch and dinners. Everyone has to calculate their own daily needs, as there is no fixed number for it. The daily requirement is calculated by age, height, athletic activity and also weight, so the demand is different for each person. As an average, however, one can say no more than 80 grams of carbohydrates per day. More than 80 grams is no longer seen as low carb.

Breakfast

Have breakfast like a king! This is your motto. In the morning you can eat a large portion of natural carbohydrates. Fresh fruit is included here, as it contains a different amount of carbohydrates in the form of fructose, depending on the fruit. Fruit provides fast energy and provides us with vitamins, fibre and minerals. Best of all, fruits are digested the fastest!

Of course, you will now say that you cannot get satisfied if you only eat some fruit! That's right! That's why you should also have protein-rich dishes for breakfast.

Fried eggs or an omelette with ingredients such as onions, peppers, tomatoes, mushrooms and herbs are wonderfully suitable. Smoked salmon is also a tasty alternative.

Need a lot of energy for the day? Eat a portion of oatmeal with fresh fruit and nut milk, or make porridge with water or milk (almond milk would be perfect too)! This gives you energy and helps you master a busy day! Coffee without sugar is allowed. Otherwise, you can also make a smoothie from fresh fruit or drink a glass of milk.

Lunch

At lunchtime, you have already used a lot of energy and you need new energy for the rest of the day. The lunch dish should consist of a large portion of vegetables. For this, you can eat low-fat meat or fish. A salad with steamed veggies and lentils or beans saturates for a long time and is also allowed on the menu.

A good lunch, for example, would be a salmon fillet with green asparagus and kohlrabi or even a cauliflower pan with coconut milk and turmeric. Try something new and cook what you like! Drink unsweetened tea or water.

Dinner

At dinner, it is the case that carbs are dispensed with as best you can. After work has been done, you only hardly move and calories are almost no longer consumed at all. In the evening, therefore, a lot of protein and light food belongs on the table.

Salads or fried fish and steamed vegetables are good food here. Soups or "warm" salads with poultry or fish can also offer a good change here. Again, you should resort to unsweetened teas or water to quench the thirst.

And in between?

Low carb is used to be able to eat large portions of food with only a few carbohydrates. Therefore, always eat until you are full at main meals so that the hunger in between does not appear at all. And if so, it is advisable to drink a glass of water first. If this does not help, you can eat a small portion of fruit as a snack. Vegetable sticks or natural nuts are also allowed and good snacks in the low carb diet.

Keep in mind, however, that the digestive tract takes time and it works best, if you don't eat something new all the time. Try to give your digestive tract at least 4-5 hours until you eat something new. Especially in the beginner's phase it is, therefore, advisable to refrain from snacks!

The 10 healthiest benefits of the Low Carb Diet

Low carb is healthy, delicious and at the same time, it keeps you fit and slim. But what else can it do?

What are the benefits of switching to low carb and what happens to your health? We would now like to introduce you to these and other benefits:

#1 Low carb curbs hunger

A lot of people know it. You go on a diet and hunger torments you for days. Not with low carb! The carbohydrate-reduced nutritional method reduces this effect, as the carbohydrates are replaced as part of the diet by proteins and fats, which pass the digestive process much slower and keep it full for a correspondingly long time.

In addition, due to the reduced intake of carbohydrates, blood sugar levels are stabilized, so that munchie attacks will not stand in the way of success!

#2 Low carb helps you lose weight

If you eat low carb, you basically lose excess pounds much faster at the beginning of the changeover than with a fat-reduced diet. This is because each gram of carbohydrates binds almost 3 grams of water to itself. It has been scientifically proven that low carb nutrition contributes a significant part to destroying excess stored water from the organism, which leads to drastic weight loss, especially in the first weeks of dietary change, and it tightens the body.

#3 Low carb also melts visceral fat

Visceral fat is the stored fat, which is stored in the free abdominal cavity and envelops internal organs, especially in the digestive system. It serves part of the mechanical protection of the internal organs and is not visible in contrast to the subcutaneous fatty tissue. Only from a certain amount, it becomes apparent by an enlargement of the belly volume.

The visceral fat should always have a healthy measure and this is supported by low carb nutrition. Scientific research shows that a significantly increased proportion of visceral fat can not only limit the functioning of the heart and liver but also promote insulin resistance, which can lead to significant metabolic dysfunctions.

It has been shown that low carb nutrition significantly supports the degradation process better than comparable other diets and thus also helps to prevent the occurrence of common diseases such as diabetes mellitus.

#4 Low carb lowers the fatty acids concentration in the blood

Fat molecules are known to significantly increase heart attack risk. You would now think you should reduce the consumption of fat and replace it with carbohydrates. But that is not the case! Studies show that the fatty acid level drops significantly when carbohydrate intake is reduced.

As a result, the risk of a heart attack is significantly reduced if you switch the diet to low carb.

#5 Reducing carbohydrates increases HDL cholesterol levels!

Fats (also called lipids) such as cholesterol are not soluble in water or blood. In order to be able to transport them to individual body regions, they are bound to certain proteins in the blood.

These compounds from lipids and proteins are called lipoproteins.

HDL cholesterol is the smallest lipoprotein of the body. They contain about 25% of the total cholesterol in the body.

According to current studies, being overweight in favour of HDL levels reduces the risk of heart attack, which is why the increase in HDL levels should be increased by means of the daily diet.
Low carb raises HDL levels significantly as there is increased consumption of fats. This is why low carb is very effective for cholesterol levels.

#6 Low carb lowers blood sugar levels

No matter what carbohydrates you consume, all of them are first broken down into glucose molecules and thus will increase the blood sugar level. This can lead to increased diabetes mellitus.
Low carb helps the body to release less insulin and thus Stabilize blood sugar levels. Snack attacks are a thing of the past.

#7 Low carb lowers blood pressure

High blood pressure usually triggers serious illnesses. Low carb has a positive effect on blood pressure, which is why the risk of strokes, heart attacks and kidney failure can be significantly reduced.

#8 Low Carb effectively fights metabolic syndrome

Metabolic syndrome is also called the "deadly quartet." It describes the combination of severe obesity, high blood pressure, insulin resistance and fat metabolism disorders.
Every single component of the syndrome has a significant impact on the health of the whole organism, which is why it should be tackled by all means. The Low Carb Nutrition, which is used to reduce the expression of each of the symptoms can also be used effectively in the context of metabolic syndrome.

#9 Low carb has a positive effect on our brain

It is true that part of the human brain only needs glucose to maintain its functions. However, this does not mean that these must be supplied by carbohydrates. The liver is also able to extract glucose from different proteins and supply the brain with it. Low carb provides the liver with these proteins and protects the body and brain from the carbohydrates it doesn't actually need at all.

#10 Low carb gives more energy and improves your skin appearance
Low carb makes you feel good and keeps fit. The heavy food of back then, which has made you feel tired and sluggish, is a thing of the past. Low carb eaters report a strongly improved skin appearance and more energy in everyday life.

Summary

Low carb is healthy, keeps fit and helps to lose weight! What are you waiting for? Get started with your own personal low carb program and enjoy the success!
As small support, we would like to introduce you again to the Do & Don'ts, which should be taken into account in the Low Carb Nutrition.

Do's and don'ts

The Do's and don'ts when it comes to a Lower Carb nutrition:

Go for it!	Leave it; Reduce it!
All the green Veggies	Sugar
(Broccoli, salad,fennel, cucumber, etc.)	honey
Pumpkin	Meat and fish with panade
Mushrooms	Liver
Tomatoes	Sausages and cold meat cuts
green, yellow, red pepper	Convenience fast food
Kale	Rice
Zucchini	Bread (made from white wheat flour)
Berries	Pasta (white wheat pasta)
Citrus fruits	Corn

Papaya	Dried fruits
Rhuburb	Grapes
Watermelon	Yoghurt
Apples	Cow milk
Cheese (organic, grassfed)	Wheat flour
Rapeseed oil, walnut oil, avocado oil, coconut oil	Balsamico Vinegar
Apple cider vinegar	Sunflower oil
Coffee (unsweetened)	Mayonnaise
Unsweetened tea	Ketchup
Tomato juice	Sweeteners
Coconut milk, almond milk (unsweetened)	Sweets
Fish (without panade)	Jam
Organic Chicken	Alcohol
Organic Meat without panade	Juice

Venison	Soft drinks
etc...	etc...

The list seems to be long but is still only a small summary of the most important foods that are or are not allowed/should be reduced at Low Carb.
Create your own dishes to your taste and eat what you really like!

I will say it again: Reduce Low carb strict during the first few weeks and then add some of your favourite Carbs (Dried fruits, bananas and oats for breakfast, potatoes, fresh juice, etc...) because our body needs healthy carbs!!

Glycemic Index

If counting calories, and refusing certain foods just because a Low Carb Guru says so is not what you want, then take a look at the Glycemic Index of food.

The glycemic index (or GI) is a ranking of carbohydrates on a scale of 0 to 100. Depending on the extent to which they increase the blood sugar level (glucose) after eating they rank in lower GI (0-55) or higher GI (55-100).

High-GI foods are those that are rapidly digested, absorbed, and metabolized, resulting in large fluctuations in blood sugar (glucose). Low GI carbs - those that cause less variation in blood sugar and insulin levels - are one of the secrets to long-term health and reduce the risk of Type 2 diabetes and heart disease. It is also known to be one of the keys to maintaining weight loss.

So I would suggest making a list to hang on your fridge/somewhere in your kitchen or have it in your handbag when you are grocery shopping to get to know the GI of your food.

While some veggies and fruits might seem to have a little too much carbs in total when you put them into a nutrition calculator, the GI might tell you it doesn't have as much sugar, so then you can decide if you want to eat it or leave it. When it comes to natural foods, I would always eat it!

Low GI Veggies examples:
Potato boiled in water: 23
Sweet potato, boiled: 44
Parsnips peeled and boiled: 52
Green banana, peeled and fried in vegetable oil: 35
Carrots, 80g, boiled: 33
Carrot, 80g raw, diced: 35
Sweet corn 80g: 55
Sweet corn on the cob, 80g, boiled 20 minutes: 48
Butternut pumpkin boiled, 80g: 51
Etc. etc.

Some low GI fruits:
Apple, raw120g (Braeburn): 32
Apple raw, 120g Golden Delicious: 39
Apricot dried, 60g: 30
Apricots halves canned in fruit juice (120g): 51
(canned has always more sugar, go for the raw or dried fruits)
Banana, ripe, all yellow 120g: 51
Oranges, raw 120g: 40

Blueberries, wild 100g: 53
Dates dried 60g (different GI on different
sorts of dried dates): From 31-50
Strawberries, 120g fresh: 40
Etc. etc.

(Source: glycemicindex.com)

So you see, a lot of variety in low GI.

Eat the rainbow, literally!

When someone says "eat the rainbow," he
doesn't mean to say you should eat those
sweets advertised with exactly this sentence
but it actually means that we should eat a
huge variety of coloured natural food. It's not
difficult to get the vitamins and nutrients you
need from a healthy, balanced diet, but it may
be difficult if you're a picky eater, or if you are
following a diet that restricts certain natural
foods.

When I scroll down IG and see that a lot of
people following a low carb diet or keto diet
are having only brown, yellow dishes, I really
feel my stomach cramp! That doesn't look like
a great variety of foods, neither very healthy.
But they either focus only on calories or just

on strict low carb: not much veggies or fruits because they contain natural sugar. Just doesn't look good and could end up in a lack of nutrients.

Colours indicate the abundance of specific nutrients. For example, yellow and orange fruits and vegetables are abundant in vitamins C and A. While green fruits and vegetables (kale, spinach, asparagus, avocado) are rich in vitamins K, B and E. Red fruits and vegetables (cabbage, grapes) are rich in vitamins C and K.

Plants often derive their colour of various phytochemicals that occur in them. These chemicals will provide you with different nutrients when consumed. This is the root of the "eating of the rainbow".

In short, eat a variety of vitamins and minerals without putting in too much effort, just look for a variety of colours.

Conclusion

Low Carb is THE trend all over the world and has already captivated thousands of people. And now it's your turn too!

In our guide, you have learned everything you need to know about low carb and are now a real expert.

Start by anchoring low carb in your head. Imagine the many health and, above all, useful principles and store them in your mind. A positive attitude to the topic is the first step in the right direction.

Then grab your very own personal "Bad Food – Box" and throw all the foods that are high in carbohydrates. Just don't forget anything, so you don't fall back on it in the event of hot hunger attacks! Please don't throw away the food, give it to friends or family or donate it to a nonprofit. In doing so, you are not only doing something good for you but also helping others.

Done?

Your next steps

Step 1: Enjoy your new grocery shopping experience

Sit down, take our list of "basics that must not be missing" and write your very own shopping list. Then head to the supermarket and start preparing for your new life. Don't forget to avoid the "nasty" stuff with the bad carbohydrates, it could tempt you especially in the beginning!

The shopping cart is full? Then off to the checkout! You will see that if you leave the convenience food on the shelves, low carb is even something for the little wallet!
Once at home, you now have your cupboards full of healthy foods and you can enjoy all the delicious things, which are also good for your health.

Step 2: Plan your week ahead of time

Now sit down again and plan your week. Set fixed meal times and don't forget to plan exercise units. Maybe you can check the tyre pressure of the bike tyres after that so that you can start to bike to work the next morning already? Or you can undust the running shoes to walk your child to kindergarten and then run the way back.

Planning exercise is easy and does not always require a visit to a gym or any classes.

Step 3: Set yourself up for success

Now get your recipes and plan your meals. If you have a busy schedule it would be a good idea to try meal prepping. Sometimes it is a good idea to cook for several days in advance and freeze the food. For example, if you have a tight daily schedule, it can happen that you have little time to prepare a meal. Before you fall into stress and grab convenience food, you'd better always have something healthy prepared.

Step 4: Enjoy real food, don't say no to natural foods

When it comes to health and nutrition, it's important to remember that focusing on one thing only is generally a bad idea. For most people, you get the nutrients you need as long as you eat a balanced diet, in a form your body can use.

It is easy to focus too much on terms like low carb or keto or high carbs or low fat and what you can't or shouldn't eat and sadly avoid the

ultimate goal this way- a balanced diet with fresh, varied products!
Just remember:

1. Eat natural food.
2. and refuse unhealthy carbs, highly processed and convenience food. At least reduce them massively and just eat them once in a while as a treat.

So, once you have put together your individual meal plan, you can start!

Start a new section of your life and step into a low carb life, which will boost your well-being and also your health.

Low carb is suitable and easy for everyone to implement. Be patient, stay focused and set small goals so you can quickly reap success.
Thousands of people have already started a new way of life with Low Carb and from now on we would like to welcome you into the circle of these people!

Use our guide in the sense of an idea box. Always take out what you need and if you struggle with something check the chapters to get answers.

From A like Atkins diet to S like sugar building blocks, you'll find everything you need to know in this little book!

We wish you great success on your exciting journey and hope that you too will soon be able to say happily and confidently: "I have achieved a new way of life!"

A few Low-Carb Recipes as inspiration:

Breakfast inspirations:

Baked Avocado

Nutritional values per serving: 530 cal, 21,1g carbs, 14g protein, 40g fat

Ingredients for 1 servings:
1 ripe Avocado
1 tbsp tabasco or soy sauce
1 tbsp lime juice
5 tbsp parmesan
salt and pepper

Instructions:
Preheat oven to 400 degrees F.
Halve the avocado and take out the kernel.
With a knife cut a checkered pattern into the Avocado, then pour the tabasco or soy sauce and lime juice on top, season with some salt and pepper. Then add 2 tbsp of parmesan into the kernel holes. Put the avocado into the oven and bake for 3 minutes. Then add the last spoon of parmesan and let bake for another

1-2 minutes until the cheese is nice golden brown.
If you like add some fresh lime juice on top before enjoying this breakfast.

You can fill the Avocado with other stuff too if you like, or bake an egg in the avocado too. Then just make sure to make the kernel hole a little bit bigger.

Crepe with crispy bacon (or tofu)

Nutrition facts per serving with bacon:
339.7 Kcal, 3.3g KH, 24.3g EW, 24.4g fat

Ingredients for 2 servings:
Dough:
4 eggs
0.25 cups almond milk (unsweetened)
1 tbsp fine coconut flour
1 tbsp flaxseed meal
¼ tsp salt
2 tbsp herbs of your choice
a little coconut oil to sauté

Filling:
4 thin slices of organic bacon (or tofu, or vegan bacon aka coconut chips)
4 cocktail tomatoes

½ red onion cut into thin slices

Instructions:
First fry the bacon, onions and tomatoes.
Bacon has to be crispy, onions and tomatoes
are allowed to turn brownish.
For the dough, mix all the ingredients in a
mixing bowl with a large fork until no lumps
are left.
Let the dough set briefly (this will make the
dough a little firmer) and stir well before use.
Heat a coated pan with a little coconut oil.
Add half of the dough to the pan and, by lifting
and twisting the pan, distribute it nicely so
that a very thin crepe is produced. Sauté
briefly until it turns slightly brown. Then put
on a plate and fill with bacon or tofu, onions
and tomatoes and roll up.
The filling is also great avocado or guacamole,
hummus or rocket salad. Or make your own
jam without extra sugar...

Frittata with goat's cheese, ham/tofu and spinach

Nutrition facts per serving:
450.1 cal, 4.6 g carbs, 32.6 g protein, 38.2 g fat

Ingredients for 2 servings:
2 tbsp olive oil
½ small onion, finely chopped
2 slices of organic ham/tofu, finely chopped
salt and pepper
¼ cup baby spinach
5 eggs, whisked
¼ cup goat cheese, diced
Optional: small side salad of your choice

Instructions:
Preheat the oven to 400 degrees F.
In an oven-proof pan, heat 1 tablespoon of oil over medium heat and stir in the onion cubes with the ham and salt and pepper until light brown.
Add the spinach and let it heat for 1-2 minutes.
Add the egg mixture, sprinkle with cheese and cook until the mixture begins on the outside to get stuck (about 1-2 minutes).
Then place in the oven and bake until the mixture becomes firm. About 10-12 minutes.

Arrange on a plate to serve and optionally add a salad.

Lunch and dinner inspirations:

Cauliflower curry

Nutritional values per serving: 147 cal, 20,6g carbs, 8.5 g protein, 2,9g fat

<u>Ingredients for 4 servings:</u>
2 tablespoons of coconut oil
1 onion, finely chopped
1 garlic clove, finely chopped
1 piece of ginger (about 2 cm) grated
2 teaspoon ground coriander
2 teaspoon ground cumin
1/3 cup of dry red lentils
1 cup vegetable broth
1 tbsp coconut oil
1 small head of cauliflower, cut into small florets
1.5 cups of coconut milk
2/3 cups frozen or fresh peas
1 handful of fresh spinach

2 tablespoons fresh coriander, chopped
1 tbsp lemon juice

Instructions:
In a deep pan or a large pot, heat the oil and sauté the onion for about 2-3 minutes.
Add the garlic, ginger, coriander, cumin and sauté for about 1-2 minutes to get the flavor out. Then add the lentils, fill with broth and bring everything to a boil. Turn down the heat and simmer for about 10 minutes. Stir in between.
Meanwhile, heat 1 tbsp of coconut oil in a non-stick pan and simmer the cauliflower for 2-3 minutes on low heat until the cabbage gets a nice color. Then add the cauliflower to the lentils and simmer the coconut milk for another 10 minutes. Finally, add the beans / peas and spinach and simmer for 3 minutes. The curry should be thickened and the vegetables are cooked, then the curry is ready.
Stir in the coriander and lemon juice at the end and season with salt and pepper.
Who likes gives a dollop of sour cream to the curry to serve.

Cauliflower hash-browns

Nutritional values per serving: 334 cal, 8.9g carbs, 12.1g proteins, 26.6g fat

Ingredients for 4:
1 small head cauliflower (minced or grated)
3 eggs
½ onion, grated
1 teaspoon salt, a little pepper
110g butter for frying

Instructions:
Mix the cauliflower with the other ingredients (without the butter) in a bowl and stir well.
Melt a generous amount of butter or oil over medium heat in a large saucepan to sauté the hash browns. Also heat your stove in a small heat to keep the first hash browns warm while doing the rest.
Add the cauliflower mixture to the pan and smooth it gently until it measures about 7-8 cm in diameter.
Fry for 4-5 minutes on low heat on each side. Have some patience when turning the pancakes. If you turn them too soon or too fast they can break.

Chili sin carne

Nutrition facts per serving:
123 cal, 20.6g carbs, 6.8g protein, 1.3g fat

Ingredients for 2 servings:
2 cups tomatoes, diced
2 medium carrots, cut into pieces
1 zucchini, cut into small pieces
1 small onion, roughly cut
2 small garlic cloves, finely chopped
1 yellow pepper, diced
1 red chilli, gutted and finely sliced
0.5 cups vegetable broth
3 tablespoons tomato paste
a little oil, salt and pepper to taste

Instructions:
Prepare all ingredients.
Heat a pan on medium heat and add some oil to the pan. Then fry the onions, chilli, garlic and tomato paste. Add the carrots, zucchini and peppers and sauté until soft.
Add the tomatoes and fill with broth, do not immediately add the whole broth, the consistency should not be too liquid.
Simmer until the veggies are cooked through. If it gets a bit too firm, add some more liquid. Stir regularly so it can not burn.

Season with salt and pepper and serve in deep plates.
If you want, you can add a dollop of sour cream on top.

Baked fish

Nutrition facts per serving:
192 cal, 4g carbs, 31.4g protein, 4.9g fat

Ingredients for 4 servings:
4 pieces of fish fillets (for example tilapia)
1 egg
0.125 cups of milk
3/10 cup freshly grated Parmesan
0.210 cups of spelt flour
Salt, pepper and paprika powder
1 lemon, divided into quarters

Instructions:
Preheat the oven to 340 degrees F.
Whisk egg and milk together and set aside in a deep dish.
In a deep plate, mix the Parmesan, the flour and some salt, pepper and paprika powder and then dip the fillets first into the egg mixture (both sides) and then into the flour mixture.
Place on a baking sheet lined with baking paper and bake for about 25 minutes (until the fish is cooked).

Serve with the lemon.

As an optional side dish: green salad, bean salad or broccoli vegetables.

Gazpacho

Nutritional values per serving: 183.6 cal, 15.3g carbs, 3.5g protein, 11.4g fat

Ingredients for 6 servings:
1 big green pepper
1 big red pepper
1 small red onion
2 small ripe avocados
4 tomatoes
2 cloves of garlic
Juice of half a lemon
fresh basil (about 3 tablespoons chopped)
1 cucumber
olive oil

Instructions:
Preheat oven to 400 degrees F. Halve the pepper and put it on a tray lined with baking paper in the oven. Bake approximately 20 min until the skin gets small black blisters.

Meanwhile, peel the onions and garlic, cut in half and place in the blender. Quarter the tomatoes. Peel and core the avocado. Give everything to the onion and the garlic.

When the peppers are ready to roast, we let them cool a bit to skin them.

With the herbs, lemon juice, salt and pepper and a tablespoon of olive oil in the blender and now we mix everything until we have a nice creamy consistency.

Finally, cut the cucumber into small pieces and mix everything together again. Season again and drizzle some olive oil over it to serve. Optionally you can sprinkle feta cheese or fresh herbs over it.

Tom Kha Gai Soup

Nutrition facts per serving:
478 cal, 11.4g carbs, 27g protein, 36g fat

Ingredients for 2 servings:
14 oz of coconut milk
0,4 pounds chicken breast (cut into bite-sized pieces) or Tofu
1 ⅓ cups mushrooms
0,6 cups of vegetables or chicken broth
2 bars of lemongrass
1 small piece of ginger, cut into very thin slices
1 red chilli pepper
some soy sauce
1 lime
Fresh coriander

Instructions:

For this Thai soup, first beat the lemongrass softly (with a meat tenderizer or a rolling pin) so that the aroma can develop better.

Put the broth and half of the coconut milk in a saucepan and bring to a boil.

Cut the lemongrass into large pieces and add the ginger to the broth in the pot. Add the whole chilli and simmer for about 10 minutes over medium heat.

Cut mushrooms into bite-sized pieces and add to the pot. Simmer for another 5 minutes.

Now add the chicken and cook for another 5-6 minutes until the meat is completely through.

Finally, add the remaining coconut milk and season with the lime juice and the soy sauce. Garnish with fresh coriander leaves.

Do not eat lemongrass and chili pepper. Either remove before serving or pick it out while eating.

Baking and desserts

Cloud bread

Nutritional facts per Oopsie Bread (1 of 6): 66 cal, 0.5g carbs, 4.8g protein, 4.6g fat

Ingredients for 6 Cloud breads:
3 organic eggs
3 tablespoons cream cheese (room temperature)
¼ tsp baking powder

Instructions:
Preheat the oven to 300 degrees F. Separate the eggs in two bowls. Mix the egg yolk with the room temperature warm cream cheese until everything is creamy. Then we sift the baking powder over it and stir it quickly under the dough.
Beat the egg whites until stiff with a pinch of salt, then slowly fold in portions of the egg yolk mass under the egg white until well blended and no yellow streaks are visible.
Lay out baking paper on the baking tray and place 6 dough "blobs" on the paper with a large spoon. If you like sprinkle a few more spices on it (for example oregano, rosemary, poppy seeds)

Approximately Bake for 25 minutes.

Coconut Energy Balls

Nutrition facts per piece:
284 cal, 2g carbs, 3.74 g protein, 27.9 g fat

Ingredients for 10 pieces:
3 ⅓ cups coconut flakes
⅞ cups whole almonds
⅓ cup coconut oil
some sweetener of your choice
a little fresh vanilla

Instructions:
First, puree the almonds in a blender.
Then gently heat the coconut oil until it is liquid.
Add coconut flakes, vanilla and warmed coconut oil to the pureed almonds and mix well. Sweet to personal taste. Try if it tastes good without additional sweetness. That would be perfect;)
Now form little balls out of this mass and roll in the coconut flakes.
Then cool the balls for a few hours and then enjoy as a snack in between.

Optional: you can add some matcha powder, or chia seeds, etc.

If you are not strictly low carb you can also blend some dates with the almond as a sweetener.

Brownies

Nutritional values per serving: 330 cal, 3.7g carbs, 10.7g protein, 29.1g fat

Ingredients for 9 servings:
¼ cups dark chocolate chips unsweetened
3 tbsp baking cocoa
1 cup butter
1 ½ cup almond flour
4 eggs
0.9 cup xylitol sugar
⅛ cup whole almonds
¼ cup of chopped walnuts
1 tsp baking powder

Instructions:
First preheat the oven to 350 degrees F (circulating air) and grease the baking pan.
Chop the walnuts and almonds roughly and set aside.
Break the chocolate into pieces, dice the butter and melt both in a hot water bath. Allow to cool slightly, but do not get stiff.
Beat the eggs with the xylith until frothy. Mix the flour, cocoa and baking powder well and

stir well with the egg and butter mixture using a hand mixer.

Finally, lift the nuts into the dough. Put everything into the greased baking pan. Bake for about 15-20 minutes. After 10 minutes make a toothpick test. Those who like their brownies a bit juicier, you take them out of the oven earlier if not leave them for a few more minutes.

Allow to cool and sprinkle some sugar dust over it (you can also make it yourself if you mix xylitol sugar in the mixer for a long time until the sugar dust develops).

Chia pudding:

Nutritional values: 117.9 cal, 9.1 g carbs, 3.9 g protein, 7g fat

Ingredients for 1 glass:
6 oz coconut milk
2 tablespoons of chia seeds
½ tsp vanilla

Instructions:
Mix all ingredients in a glass or bowl.
Put the lid on the glass or cover the bowl with a plate and put the glass into the fridge. Let soak overnight or for at least 4 hours.

Serve the chia pudding with fresh fruits

Chocolate nuts

Nutritional information for one serving: 93 cal, 3.6g carbs, 4.2g protein, 5.9g fat

Ingredients for about 15 small portions:
1 cup whole almonds (or cashews or macadamia nuts (unsalted)) or if you like use a nut mix.
1 bar of chocolate, sugar-free!

Instructions:
Put the almonds, or the nut mix into a high-performance blender and chop a little, not too small, we want to have larger pieces.
Then melt the chocolate in a water bath.
If the chocolate is liquid, we add the nut pieces into the melted chocolate, take out small portions with two spoons and place them on baking paper to cool and let them dry.

About the author

Living on a vegetarian diet for 29 years, and on a dairy free lower carb diet for almost 4 years now.

"Since I stopped buying plastic wrapped food, it got much easier to hold my weight. I feel fitter because I leave the unhealthy, processed, convenience food in the store naturally:)"